D0209091

"Imagined or otherwise, intrigue in Silicon Valley rarely fails to fascinate. Wendy Goldman Rohm and Bob Young have recreated an engrossing account about the birthing of a movement that is shaking the very foundations of computing as we know it today.

"Anyone fascinated by the continuing saga of the world's most important industry will appreciate this book."

—Heather Clancy, Editor, *Computer Reseller News*

"Years from now, we'll recall how Bill Gates's empire crumbled. When that day arrives, this eloquent book will explain to all, in brilliant fashion, the beginning of the end."

—E.J. Gong, hi-tech columnist, ABCNEWS.com

"With *Under the Radar*, Wendy Goldman Rohm and Bob Young have created a very interesting tale and a pacesetting book. First, we had general books about getting rich. Then, books about getting rich in Silicon Valley. Now we have stories about how companies get rich—or at least how they succeed in a hostile business. Recommended."

—John C. Dvorak, *PC Magazine*

"Rohm and Young's surprising insider account is required reading for anyone who thinks that the software wars are over. This fast-paced saga provides a first-hand account of a small-time, small-town company thrust into the mega-million-dollar whirlwind world of high-tech finance and strategy, to emerge much bigger than even they had ever imagined. And that's only the beginning."

—Rebecca Lynn Eisenberg, high tech columnist and consultant,
   San Francisco Examiner, CBS.MarketWatch

"Wendy Goldman Rohm and Bob Young have written a thriller. Their fast-paced account of how Linux is subverting the trillion dollar software industry reads more like Grisham than computer code. It will send shivers down readers' necks, especially if they are called Bill Gates."

—Daniel Jeffreys, *London Daily Mail*

"Bob Young and Wendy Goldman Rohm have created a clear narrative describing the most important development in computing this decade: the emergence of Linux. In *Under The Radar*, we learn that Linux didn't emerge all by itself."

—Paul E. Schindler Jr., Editor, *Byte.com*

under
the radar

All royalties earned are being donated to the Free Software
Foundation to further its important work.

How Red Hat Changed
the Software Business—
and Took Microsoft
by Surprise

Robert Young, CEO of Red Hat
&
Wendy Goldman Rohm

President, CEO
Keith Weiskamp

Publisher
Steve Sayre

Acquisitions Editor
Stephanie Wall

Marketing Specialist
Diane Enger

Project Editor
Michelle Stroup

Production Coordinator
Jon Gabriel

Cover Design
Jesse Dunn

Layout Design
April Nielsen

Under The Radar
© 1999 The Coriolis Group. All Rights Reserved.

This book may not be duplicated in any way without the express written consent of the publisher, except in the form of brief excerpts or quotations for the purposes of review. The information contained herein is for the personal use of the reader and may not be incorporated in any commercial programs, other books, databases, or any kind of software without written consent of the publisher. Making copies of this book or any portion for any purpose other than your own is a violation of United States copyright laws.

Limits Of Liability And Disclaimer Of Warranty
The author and publisher of this book have used their best efforts in preparing the book and the programs contained in it. These efforts include the development, research, and testing of the theories and programs to determine their effectiveness. The author and publisher make no warranty of any kind, expressed or implied, with regard to these programs or the documentation contained in this book.

The author and publisher shall not be liable in the event of incidental or consequential damages in connection with, or arising out of, the furnishing, performance, or use of the programs, associated instructions, and/or claims of productivity gains.

Trademarks
Trademarked names appear throughout this book. Rather than list the names and entities that own the trademarks or insert a trademark symbol with each mention of the trademarked name, the publisher states that it is using the names for editorial purposes only and to the benefit of the trademark owner, with no intention of infringing upon that trademark.

The Coriolis Group, LLC
14455 N. Hayden Road
Suite 220
Scottsdale, Arizona 85260

480/483-0192
FAX 480/483-0193
http://www.coriolis.com

Library of Congress Cataloging-in-Publication Data
Young, Robert, 1952-
    Under the radar: how Red Hat changed the software business--and took Microsoft by surprise/by Robert Young and Wendy Goldman Rohm.
        p. cm.
    Includes index.
    ISBN 1-57610-506-7
    1. Red Hat, Inc. 2. Microsoft Corporation. 3. Linux.
4. Computer software industry--United States. I. Rohm, Wendy Goldman. II. Red Hat, Inc.. III. Title.
HD9696.63.U64R439 1999
338.7'610053'0973--dc21
                                                                99-43074
                                                                    CIP

1   2   3   4   5   6   7   8   9   10

To everyone who has ever contributed so much as one line of code to an open source project.

—Robert Young

For my parents

—WGR

Table Of Contents

Acknowledgments

There are just too many people to thank for their help in creating
the story that led to this book and the book itself for me to even hope
to begin to list them all. I'm indebted to each and every one of you,
including:

Frank, the UPS driver, who quizzed my Canadian-educated daugh-
ters on their U.S. geography lessons while he waited for us to finish
packing the day's shipments out of our house in Westport, Connecti-
cut back in '94; my colleagues at Red Hat who provided the details to
the stories quoted, and who, like Lisa Sullivan, helped build the business model; software developers and users like Erik Troan, Alan Cox,
and Donald Becker who patiently explained why source code and a
license to modify it is so important; Wendy and the talented staff at
Coriolis.

All the errors and omissions are mine alone.

—Robert Young

Great appreciation and thanks for their help with this book go to
Linus Torvalds, Eric Hahn, Richard Stallman, Eric Raymond, Nancy
Young, Paul McNamara, Lisa Sullivan, and Michael Fulbright.

I also thank Jesse Dunn, Diane Enger, Jon Gabriel, Tricia McArdle,
April Nielsen, Michelle Stroup, and Stephanie Wall at Coriolis for their

great work on very tight deadlines, and Akira Kurahone, my Japanese translator who has done an incredible job on more than one of my books. I thank Bob Young for being the fascinating person he is, and for the opportunity to work with him.

Much appreciation goes to my agent, Bill Gladstone, for his enthusiasm and unflagging support.

Hugs to my wonderful daughter Madeline, who, as usual, put up with my intense deadlines and distractions, and to my friends Bibi Tinsley, Gail Richman, S.L. Daniels, Ric Murphy, and Josip Pasic.

—Wendy Goldman Rohm

Foreword

Hardware evolves faster than software. This is a known truth of the information industry—at least since I got into it in 1976, and probably before. No one was ever able to explain to me why this was so, it just was. Moore's Law, that processor speeds would double every 18 months, only applied to processors. There was no equivalent in software productivity. At least until today. The open source software development movement promises to do for software development what transistors did for computer hardware.

The most common question I'm asked is: How can a software development model that is dependent on a bunch of kids hacking code in their basements be reliable and scalable enough to challenge technology giants like IBM, Sun Microsystems, and even Microsoft?

We've attempted to answer that question in as short and concise a manner as we could by pulling examples of the professional engineering teams who have been contributing to the inventory of open software, and examples of the recent acceleration in the open source software development projects and movement generally.

The examples may not be convincing enough in themselves, but keep in mind these are all just examples. There are hundreds, if not thousands, of projects we could have used in each and every instance. If you don't like the examples we used, please don't hesitate to do your own research. With little effort you'll be able to find dozens of other, perhaps better examples.

This is not a history book. It is meant to be an illustration of a business model. As such we made no effort to be comprehensive, just to use some stories to illustrate what is a remarkable movement to bring the computer software industry into the new millennium.

The inspiration for this book was a speech I gave at the Waterside publishing conference in April this year. It was an odd speech as I'd been on a sales tour and had come down with a classic case of laryngitis. I could not speak above a whisper an hour before the speech, but with lots of coffee I managed to croak out some ideas on how free software was a lot like free speech. Red Hat's success was due in no small part to our willingness to try to fundamentally change the rules of the industry in which we were participating.

The tape of the speech that Bill Gladstone, literary agent and head of Waterside Productions, sent to Wendy Goldman Rohm to attempt to convince her to co-author a book on the subject, suffered from my lack of voice to such an extent that she could not understand it. She insisted that I spend an hour on the phone reciting it to her. Of course I never write my speeches, so I doubt my recollection of that speech bore more than a passing resemblance to the one that I gave to the conference, but it must have been interesting enough in its own right to convince Wendy to give up three months of her life to work on this project.

The gist of that speech was that the traditional proprietary software development model was a lot like the old feudal systems. Software was developed by small teams of engineers who maintained control over the users of their products by keeping tight control over the technology. The users did not have any freedom in their use of the software technology on which they depended.

Open source looks a lot more like how modern free market-based democratic societies work. All of us have the opportunity to build on the knowledge and contributions of those who have gone before in an open, free society.

Russ Nelson, a leading member of the open source community, has pointed out that the term "the continuing revolution" is an oxymoron. Either a revolution succeeds, in which case the revolutionary concepts becomes part of the established rules of society, or it fails and becomes a footnote in history. The open source movement stands today at the brink of losing its status as a revolution by Nelson's insightful definition.

Wendy has done a wonderful job of conveying the sense of adventure and excitement that it has been my privilege to have shared over the last five years with talented colleagues at Red Hat, and all our friends in the open source industry.

Yet her principle contribution was to ensure that this was not a narrow view of this movement. By tracking down and interviewing Linus Torvalds, Larry McVoy, Eric Hahn, Miguel Icaza and numerous other key contributors to this movement, she brings to this book a very broad perspective of the movement.

Since this is not a history book, let me apologize to all those open source community developers and friends, as well as my co-conspirators at Red Hat. They are doing, and have done, so much to make the open source software movement a success, yet not all are mentioned in this short book. Someday, perhaps, we may write the book that attempts to give everyone their just recognition, but this is not that book.

Bob Young, July 1999

Timeline

1968

ARPANET, the Internet's precursor, is founded. Although designed to allow researchers to share code and information on projects, it also becomes a showcase for the abilities of open-source software.

1969

Ken Thompson, a researcher at Bell Labs, writes the first version of Unix, a multiuser, multitasking operating system. The Unix source code is distributed freely throughout the '70s, and it soon becomes popular at universities and research labs.

1971

Richard Stallman, a pioneer in the open-source movement, joins an MIT group devoted exclusively to free software. The developer of the first Emacs text editor, Stallman later founds the GNU project (short for GNU's Not Unix); this leads to the creation of a free, Linux-based operating system.

1973

Vinton Cerf and Bob Kahn from DARPA (Defense Advanced Research Projects Agency) develops the TCP/IP protocol, which becomes the networking foundation of the Internet. A decade later, the Department of Defense christens the Internet and mandates that all computers attached to the Internet use TCP/IP.

1979

AT&T announces plans to commercialize Unix. This leads the University of California at Berkeley to create its own version of Unix, called BSD (Berkeley Software Distributions) Unix. BSD Unix is adopted by early commercial vendors such as DEC and Sun. AT&T and Sun later agree to merge their versions of Unix, prompting competitors (DEC, HP, and IBM) to form the Open Software Foundation.

A student at the University of California at Berkeley, Eric Allman, develops a program to route messages between computers over ARPANET. Allman later evolves the program into Sendmail. Today, more than 75 percent of Internet email servers use this open-source program to deliver mail.

1983

In a reaction to the proprietary trend in software, Stallman establishes the GNU project to promote the free-software model by developing a free operating system, applications, and programming tools. More important, GNU establishes the General Public License (GPL), better known as a copyleft, which becomes the model for many open-source projects.

1986

Larry Wall creates Perl (Practical Extraction and Report Language), a versatile programming language used for writing CGI (Common Gateway Interface) scripts, which are the standard means of delivering more dynamic content on the Web today.

1987

Developer Andrew Tanenbaum releases Minix, a version of Unix for the PC, Mac, Amiga, and Atari ST. It comes with complete source code.

1991

Aiming to exceed the capabilities of Minix, a young student at the University of Helsinki, Linus Torvalds, releases operating system kernel. Three years later, Torvalds copylefts Linux. Today, there are an estimated 10 to 20 million Linux users.

1993

FreeBSD 1.0 is released. Based on BSD Unix, FreeBSD includes networking, virtual memory, task switching, and large filenames. The BSD license does not require developers to give anything back.

1995

Marc Ewing and Bob Young form Red Hat Software, Inc. to address Linux's system administration ease-of-use problems. Red Hat packages Linux with third-party applications, documentation, and initial technical support and sells it for about $50. Red Hat quickly becomes the leading Linux-based operating system supplies.

Bryan Sparks founds Caldera with backing by former Novell CEO Ray Noorda.

The Apache Group builds a new Web server, Apache, based on the National Center for Supercomputing Applications' (NCSA's) HTTPd 1.3 and a series of patch files. The free Web server becomes one of the most popular HTTP servers.

1997

Eric S. Raymond, programmer and author of The New Hacker's Dictionary, delivers a paper titled "The Cathedral and the Bazaar," contrasting commercial and open-source development models, at Linux Kongres. The paper helps inspire Netscape's Mozilla.org.

August 1997

In investment round "A," Red Hat gets $2 million from Frank Batten Jr.

January 1998

Fermilab officially chooses Red Hat Linux as one of its operating systems.

February 1998

Netscape announces it will not only give away Communicator 5.0 but will also release its source code.

Fall 1998

Major software vendors, including Computer Associates, Corel, IBM, Informix, Interbase, Oracle, and Sybase, announce plans to port their products to Linux.

November 1998

Mired in a landmark antitrust case, Microsoft issues a statement citing Linux as evidence that the company does not have a monopoly on operating systems. Shortly afterward, the Halloween documents—a series of internal Microsoft memoranda on the threats posed by open-source software and Linux—are leaked to the open-source community and posted on the Web.

Sun Microsystems announces plans to release the source code for Java 2 (formerly known as JDK 1.2) to developers, under a modified license.

February 1998

Red Hat meeting in Portland, Oregon with a workstation software group who were considering porting math libraries to Linux at the request of Fermilab and Brookhaven.

Bob Young's first meeting with Netscape regarding licensing open source.

March 1998

Red Hat receives calls from 13 different people at Intel working on 8 different teams, all of whom claim to be the only ones at Intel who understand the potential importance of the Linux-based operating systems to Intel.

Tim "Wookie" Witham, from Intel, meets with Bob Young and Erik Troan at Red Hat's offices.

April 1998

Red Hat meets with Intel's Scott Richardson and his staff. Present are Eric Troan, Donnie Barnes, Marc Ewing, and Bob Young.

Bob meets with Netscape. In attendance, John Paul, Senior VP server engineering; Marc Andreessen; and three others.

Benchmark first meeting (lunch on Sand Hill Road).

May 1998

A Red Hat team sits down with a team of Intel's business development team, including Andre Turenne, Alan Holtzman and others who sketch out exactly what they would like from Red Hat. Intel had no strategy to deal with Linux being shipped and used by its customers.

All of the meeting's discussion is so far beyond its own goals or expectations, that Red Hat execs walked out just shaking their heads.

Red Hat hires Paul McNamara, an ex-IBM executive who is assigned to spearhead the Intel relationship.

Red Hat commits one-quarter of its development budget to Gnome development and GTK libraries.

June 1998

Red Hat meeting with Intel, in which Intel explains how its investment process works. It requires the participation of a leading VC.

A few days prior to Intel meeting, Bob Young gets a call from Kevin Harvey of Benchmark, a call that Kevin explains later as the "only cold-call he has ever made as a venture capitalist."

Hahn quits Netscape after 18 months there.

July 1998

Benchmark introduces Greylock to Red Hat.

Marc Ewing and Bob Young fly up to Boston to meet Bill Kaiser of Greylock, who Kevin Harvey wants to bring into the investment round. Kaiser's reaction is to question why we need the venture capitalists at all. While he later insists that he was being sincere and that this was not just a very effective sales technique, it was a very effective sales technique, which causes Marc and Bob to convince Kaiser that they wanted his help. Greylock later helps recruit Red Hat president Matthew Szulik.

Benchmark and Greylock attempt to convince Red Hat to let them invest first, and then to later, at a presumably higher price, bring the corporate investors into Red Hat. Not unexpectedly, Intel expresses extreme displeasure with this idea.

September 1998

Bob had been involved in some difficult closings before, but the chess game strategies that were required to convince all of Red Hat's existing shareholders and the four new investors to sign the same pieces of paper to get this deal closed was without doubt the most difficult negotiations he'd ever been involved in. It closed with only hours to spare the day before the major announcement that was scheduled at the ISPCON industry conference.

Netscape, Intel, Greylock, Benchmark investment announced.

February 1999

Dell certification of Linux announced.

IBM partnership announced.

March 1999

Compaq, IBM, Novell, and Oracle investment announced.

April 1999

Dell investment and preloading of Linux announcement. Also, Red Hat announces Red Hat Linux 6.0 with Linux 2.2 kernel.

May 1999

Hahn joins Red Hat board.

—1—

Inside The Tent

*"I actually think that operating systems should be invisible.
People should take them for granted."*

—Linus Torvalds

THERE WAS A BLIP ON THE SCREEN, something new in the field.
At first barely visible. It had appeared slowly and almost imperceptibly. Indeed, at first it had been difficult to see there was anything at all. No, this was not some dramatic sighting, no alien mother ship suddenly blazing its way across the screen.

The first time that engineers at silicon giant Intel Corp. had the first inkling of change was when scientific labs across the country began demanding that it port its "math libraries" to a new operating system.

For one, Dr. Yeh, a Taiwanese scientist at Midwest-based Fermilab, had made such a plea in early 1998. Fermilab, the federally funded atom-smashing think tank overseen by the U.S. Department of Energy, was a mecca for the world's top nuclear physicists. It had quietly added a new flavor of system software to its roster of those driving the lab's network of computers.

Such sites were known in the computer industry as "early adopters," technically savvy users that often were the first to install leading edge products before the market had fully accepted them. One of the

1

critical benefits of the new software Fermilab had installed was that it was almost crash proof, and—even more importantly—scientists could freely tinker with its source code, the guts of any piece of software.

This was not the norm in the Microsoft-dominated software industry. Source code was like a secret chamber that few were allowed to enter. By keeping this code to themselves, software companies kept control of their customers, dictated technological change, and ensured continual revenue streams. With the source code kept secret and inaccessible, customers were locked into continual operating system upgrades dictated by the supplier. Likewise, application software creators depended on the internal workings of the operating system, and were often put at a disadvantage by the suppliers' secrecy.

"We need your math libraries to run under Linux," a number of Fermilab scientists repeatedly told Intel.

Linux. Barely a soul at Intel knew the first thing about it. To a $25 billion-a-year American corporation that had sealed off its prized programmers and engineers from the rest of the world with electronic firewalls and CIA-like security, it seemed like a seething and uncontrollable underground of hackers.

On their own, such requests would not have caused much notice inside the giant corporation and would have remained an oddity. But something startling was going on, the type of thing that made a corporation like Intel turn on a dime. Literally.

While the phones were ringing at Intel with similar requests from laboratories all over the world, the chip gods quietly perused the results of a confidential market study, and chairman Andy Grove pulled a low-profile line manager into his office.

———

Kevin Harvey was a 34-year-old stalker of fortunes.

While eyes were being opened at Intel to a subtle shift going on in the marketplace, in the spring of 1998, Harvey, one of the country's top venture capitalists, was inspired to place the first cold call he'd ever made in his career as a venture capitalist.

To see Harvey in his element, one must traverse Sand Hill Road as it winds serenely through the rolling hills of Silicon Valley, wrapping itself around a smattering of office buildings and think tanks. Many young entrepreneurs and budding superstars have navigated this route, through California's Menlo Park, to building number 2480 in the Quadrus office complex.

Here one finds the headquarters of Harvey's firm, Benchmark Capital, where elegant carpeted conference rooms belie the often frenzied venture capital activity being conducted within.

Harvey is one of the original partners at Benchmark, the red-hot high-technology venture capital company, founded in 1995, which had become the buzz of the investment community. With an amazing 100 percent annual return on its first fund, Benchmark was wowing the Valley. Investors had been lining up at the firm's door these days.

Just down Sand Hill Road were competitors like Kleiner Perkins Caufield & Byers, as well as Mayfield Capital, who were scrambling as fast as Benchmark to satisfy hungry investors looking for the next great thing.

Harvey, with his laid-back demeanor, brown hair and trim beard, was an accessible sort, and accustomed to being courted by all manner of startups. With the explosion of the Internet, the industry was going gangbusters. Just the year before, venture capital firms collectively had invested $8.4 billion in technology startups. (That was up from $5.9 billion in 1996.) Harvey's mission, like that of all venture capitalists, was to fund promising new companies in return for stock that one day might be worth a fortune.

Harvey and his partners also often recruited management talent for the companies they funded. Benchmark had been responsible for bringing chairman and CEO Jim Barksdale to Netscape, for example.

The venture capital world was about as aggressive as they come. One of Harvey's colleague's, Robert Kagle, sported a plaque above his desk: "The Broken Computer Award—Profits So Huge that they Broke the Computer." There was no other way to describe the results of some of the deals Benchmark had recently orchestrated. In 1997, it had bought 22 percent of Internet auction company eBay Inc. for $5 million. That stake, by the spring of 1999, would be worth about $2.5 billion—a 49,900 percent return on its investment. Benchmark's computers, which only record gains of up to $100 million, literally could not accept such a figure. Hence the title of the ersatz award. Each of the five Benchmark partners would enjoy about $120 million of the eBay profit.

In such an environment, needless to say, Kevin Harvey never had to make cold calls.

This time, however, was different. He'd received an interesting tip from Netscape chief technology officer Eric Hahn, who was an investor in a Benchmark fund. Hours later, Harvey picked up the phone and began to dial the number of a company he knew almost nothing about.

"Bob Young please," he said, and was rolled over to voicemail.

Back at Intel, in the spring of 1998, executives inside the company's server division in Hillsborough, Oregon, placed a flurry of phone calls trying to line up its next strategic business partner. Red flags were going up in many areas of the market. Linux was suddenly everywhere, popping up in internal marketing studies where it hadn't been sighted on any of Intel's market maps before.

Intel, the giant American success story that, together with Microsoft, had spawned a worldwide industry, was a master in monitoring changes in the marketplace and spotting innovators and potential partners for new ventures.

What was this stuff, and where was it coming from?

Linux sightings were simultaneously being noticed around the company. While Bruce Greer had been the one inside Intel to recognize that Linux was creating quite a splash in the scientific community, in a separate division, Scott Richardson was likewise surprised at a newcomer showing up on recent market studies Intel had conducted in the computer server market.

It was not lost on Intel that, in the spring of 1998, there were almost 5,000 Internet service providers (ISPs) worldwide, a number that was rapidly growing. (By the spring of 1999, that number would grow to about 14,000 ISPs, and Intel predicted that by the year 2000, there would be almost 20,000 ISPs on the planet.)

Intel had been studying the ISP market, and—being a computer architecture company whose core business was processors—it studied what computer architectures were being used inside the typical ISP. What it discovered was a very mixed variety of technologies were being used.

A curious shift in the market seemed to be occurring. Not only were ISPs running 20 percent of their servers using the Linux operating system, but Intel's own "white box" channel (thousands of computer makers worldwide who put their own brand names on systems using Intel motherboards) reported that they were selling and supporting a startling number of their machines using a nonstandard operating system. (The unsung heroes of Intel's profitability were these "white box" manufacturers. It was one of Intel's best kept secrets that this channel of distribution represented some 37 percent of PC sales worldwide—the next biggest revenue "channel" behind its largest computer-making customers like Compaq and IBM.)

Back at Intel's Santa Clara offices, according to those present, Intel chairman Andy Grove was surprised and annoyed, the combination of which caused him to toss a few profanities into his sentences.

"We need to have a Linux position!" he said. "Why the #$%$! aren't we doing something about this?"

Clearly, something different was going on. Around the same time that Intel's market studies were coming in, an Intel line manager had startled everyone, including chairman Grove, when he started showing his Linux demos around the company.

The fellow had been running Linux inside Intel as a hobbyist in experimental mode for quite some time, but no one had seemed to notice. Recently, a general manager inside the company began asking if anyone knew anything about Linux. He discovered he had an expert on his staff.

Intel's newly discovered Linux expert gave a five-minute demonstration of the technology to other Intel general managers. The enthused bosses then took their Linux man around the company to show the demo again and again to higher level executives, until finally he found himself an audience in front of chairman Andy Grove.

The implications were stunning. If this was an operating system that was powerful and reliable enough to be used to drive high-demand Internet servers, and was open to all who wished to tune it to their needs, it could have a strategic impact on the way Intel—and everyone else in the industry, for that matter—was doing business.

Executives at the highest levels at the company had long recognized that proprietary operating system manufacturers were not moving their operating systems forward as quickly as Intel was advancing microprocessor technology. That is, Intel was being held hostage by those that controlled the operating system. If it had new technology available at the processor level that would allow computer users to do new things, it had to wait until the operating system supplier decided it was willing to build support for these features into the system.

With an open source operating system, Intel could enhance the operating system itself if it so desired, to support its new chip technology. It then could contribute the enhanced software back to everyone who was using Linux, for example.

This represented the first time that operating system development might be able to keep up with the new hardware that Intel was bringing to market.

Moreover, the thought that it could itself begin to tune an operating system to take immediate advantage of any new chip technology it pleased was a very attractive one to Intel, which had been in lockstep with Microsoft for more than a decade.

Historically, Intel always had to rely on close relationships with other companies to show the marketplace the usefulness of its technology.

For example, in preparation for the launch of its Pentium III processor, Intel was working with the Internet search engine Excite far in advance to tune the service to the power of its new advances in silicon. For the launch of Pentium III, it would demonstrate a conventional search engine with a new three-dimensional display. Instead of having to click to go to the next ten pages, and click again to the next, the information was arranged on carousels that could be pulled backwards, forwards, and rotated. Instead of a URL link, Internet users would see a thumbnail showing the front page of the site.

Meantime, the flip side of such beneficial collaborations between companies bringing new technology to market was being graphically illustrated to the Department of Justice in its antitrust investigation of Microsoft. The evidence showed that Microsoft was in a position to call all the shots, often bullying its supposed business partners to limit themselves to Microsoft-owned technology. Microsoft appeared to have gone so far as to dictate how fast other companies could bring out new products—or if they could bring them out at all, for that matter.

Indeed, Intel witnesses came forward with evidence that seemed to indicate that Microsoft had forced Intel to refrain from developing certain technologies it had in its labs. Intel vice president Steven McGeady would testify that Microsoft threatened to withhold critical technical support from Intel if the chipmaker did not stop developing software that Microsoft believed competed with its own product strategies.

But Intel's eagerness to participate in the open source business had nothing to do with any animosity the chip giant had toward its partner Microsoft. Instead, Intel was about to embark on a strategic partnership that had everything to do with smart business.

Linux represented something quite different from the way Intel itself relied on proprietary operating system suppliers to support its microprocessors.

What's more, even though various versions of Linux can be obtained from numerous places on the Web, executives noticed that Intel's market studies showed that most of the Linux software being installed by its customers was coming from one company.

———

Far from the buzz of Silicon Valley, Red Hat, Inc. is tucked away amidst the second-growth pine forests, strawberry fields, and tree farms of Durham, North Carolina. On a driving tour of the area, an occasional tobacco field rolls by, an anachronism of a geography transformed by the shifting perceptions and preferences of the marketplace.

While the dwindling tobacco fields signaled the waning of a once-powerful industry, for some, the sudden appearance of our company represented just the opposite. Frank Batten Jr., our first angel investor, in 1997 saw Red Hat not just as a promising new company but the beginnings of an industry that would shake the very foundation of the existing software business.

Even to Red Hat executives, it remained to be seen whether this assessment would be visionary or pure hyperbole.

The local press had taken to calling our employees "the mad hatters." Who wouldn't? Company executives would be the first to agree that our business model appeared at first glance to be insane: making a business out of selling free software, and developing new technology that we would never own or control. On top of this, our company was competing in the operating systems market, a market controlled by a monopolist: Microsoft.

But in the spring of 1998, Red Hat executives burrowed among the hive of windowless cubicles in the center of our 10,000 square-foot office were seeing smoke signals from Silicon Valley. Business leaders there seemed to know something we did not: Our business model had begun to prove itself in the market.

In recent weeks, we had received calls from no less than thirteen different managers at Intel Corp.—leaders of eight different development teams inside the chip behemoth. Each caller claimed to be "the only one at Intel who understands the potential importance of Linux-based operating systems."

There were benefits to being geographically remote from the rest of the software industry: It allowed us to focus on our customers' needs versus doing what the industry told us was right to do. The downside, of course, was that the company had no idea how the rest of the industry viewed us. We would soon discover that the industry was paying a great deal more attention than we thought.

Quietly, since Red Hat's founding in 1993, we had focused on an approach to software development that enabled us to tap into a worldwide software development team bigger than even the biggest industry giants could afford. Our development model—which mirrored the model being used for years by hackers all over the planet—would turn out to be more effective than the conventional closed-source, proprietary model being used across the industry by leaders such as Microsoft and other software makers.

"Open source" is a methodology as much as a philosophy and a new paradigm for doing business. This approach toward building software seems to be in keeping with the underlying forces that built the Internet itself, and was in part responsible for the Internet's sudden explosion as a worldwide network used freely by all and owned by no one company or person. It offers an opportunity for anyone, anywhere to participate.

Linux was not born with Red Hat. In 1991, Finnish programmer Linus Torvalds, a 21-year-old student at the University of Helsinki, created a unifying kernel for what had been known as GNU, a free Unix-like operating system that was launched in 1984 by free software guru Richard Stallman and distributed for free over the Internet. Stallman, a resident genius hacker at Massachusetts Institute of Technology, would insist that the more accurate name for Linux would be GNU/Linux, because the kernel written by Torvalds, though perhaps the most important part of the system, is only a small percentage of a Unix-style operating system.

What enabled Torvalds to freely distribute Linux worldwide with some assurance that it would remain "open," was that he did so under the General Public License (GPL) developed by Stallman, which allowed users not only the right to download and use the software for free, but also to modify and redistribute it in a modified state for free. Rapidly, with thousands of programmers working on Linux and redistributing it via the Internet, the rate of improvements and new features for the program accelerated. While new versions of commercial software products typically are issued once a year—or even once every three years (as had been the case with Windows 98), enhancements to open-source programs like Linux were being posted monthly or even many times a month.

We recognized the value of giving customers control of their software, and sought to bring brand reliability to the Linux product. We would offer support to customers and accelerate development of the operating system by investing our own R&D dollars in new Linux technology that would then be given back for free to the community, for any Linux programmer or distributor to use. We had no intention of ever "owning" the intellectual property we created. Instead, our business model was based on quickly expanding the market, and earning a small amount of revenue from a large number of customers who would buy a product that was better quality than that being offered by the industry leader, Microsoft.

Linux is free. Anyone can download the 500 MB operating system consisting of 650 programs from the Internet. But we offer official versions of Red Hat Linux in a shrink-wrapped package for sale through retail outlets. We sell training, education, customer support, and consulting services. Such services will provide the bulk of our future profits. Customers are paying for the convenience of the retail packaging, and for the support that comes along with it.

It had been an interesting journey to the point where we won the belief of our first angel investor. Most venture capitalists who had approached us had balked at the notion of a business based on "free" software.

Back in 1995, Brad Burnham, a venture capitalist with AT&T Ventures, began talking with us, intrigued with the concept of an "open source" operating system, largely because of pressure Microsoft was putting on the industry at the time.

Microsoft had been pushing its new online service, The Microsoft Network (MSN), and Burnham had explained to me that all the media companies were terrified of MSN. If the Internet became The Microsoft Network, they reasoned, Microsoft would own the subscribers and would reduce the media companies to being mere content providers for Microsoft subscribers. They were panicked by the idea.

In the course of doing research for AT&T Ventures to determine whether there was some model for keeping these technologies from being owned by Microsoft, Burnam became intrigued with our alternative operating system.

In the end, two things prevented a deal from going forward. AT&T Ventures is a focused venture fund interested primarily in funding telecom technologies. Red Hat isn't a telecom company. AT&T Ventures is also an East Coast, conservative operation. Although Burnham told us that he would have funded Red Hat at the outset, he was never able to get his partners to take us seriously.

Burnham urged us, however, to talk to Dave Richardson, the CEO of Infinet, a Norfolk, Virginia ISP that sold wholesale Internet services to large newspaper chains such as the Philadelphia Enquirer. After speaking with us, Richardson commented that although Red Hat was "interesting," we were too small.

"You should talk to one of our investors," Richardson kindly urged. "He'll look at things other people think are crazy. He wants to invest in new industries, versus new companies."

Indeed, just as we were getting used to rejection, Frank Batten Jr. (Richardson's investor) recognized that Red Hat was first in a potentially significant new industry. Batten was with Landmark Communication, a big investment fund also operating out of Norfolk, Virginia. (Landmark's most famous investment was the Weather Channel, and it had taken Landmark ten years to completely understand the economic model for that successful business.) Batten's philosophy is to invest in the first company of a new industry, because, if it's well funded, it will become one of the major players in that industry.

From the fall of 1996 to August 1997, Batten engaged in continual talks with us about our business model and development. As the talks with Batten went on, we were receiving signals that we were on the right track. Our unconventional business model was in fact proving itself in the marketplace.

On the evening of Sunday, February 1, 1997, at about 11 p.m., Red Hat cofounder Marc Ewing was cruising around the Internet. That winter evening, Ewing logged onto Infoworld.com, the Web site for computer-industry newspaper Infoworld, to discover we had won the Infoworld product of the year award for operating systems. We had won the award along with Microsoft. It was a tie between Red Hat Linux and Microsoft's Windows NT.

At the time, there were a total of 20 employees at Red Hat including receptionists, sales, and administrative staff. The astounding thing was, the best the company's $30-billion-dollar competitor could do—with several thousand of the world's best software developers, a virtually unlimited budget, and a three-year head start—was to tie Red Hat for this award.

That award truly belonged to the whole open source development community that had contributed the code and tools used to build Red Hat Linux.

The success of Linux should not have been a surprise: It was almost inevitable. The Linux software development team was in fact bigger than anything even Microsoft could afford, and the software development model behind it was more effective than the conventional closed-source proprietary model.

This model was working so well it attracted the initial interest of a large number of the leading venture capitalist companies besides AT&T

Ventures. From 1995 to 1997, we had had calls from several of these, including Summit, Accel Partners, and Menlo Ventures, and the calls all went the same way. The venture capitalists would introduce themselves, congratulate us on our success that they'd heard about in their research, and ask us how we'd managed to become the leading trusted supplier of open-source software. I'd explain that it was our commitment to publishing every line of code we wrote, and the benefits this gave to our users. The venture capitalists would then say something like, "Wow, that's fascinating. Well, best of luck to you—but don't call us, we'll call you." I'd never hear from them again.

By August 1997, Batten had committed to a $2 million dollar investment, which enabled us to take the company to the next level.

By the spring of 1998, the voice of Benchmark Capital fortune hunter Kevin Harvey was among the messages waiting in my voice mailbox. At the same time, we were being courted by Intel Corp., and our tiny management team was preparing for a critical tête-à-tête with the chip giant.

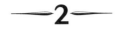

Hotbed

"For companies like Intel and other companies that were set up before the Internet, it has been an unavoidable challenge for us to adjust our business models and try to take advantage of the Internet."

—Sean Maloney, Intel corporate vice president

IN THE SPRING OF 1998, Red Hat stood between two worlds: the avant garde universe of rebel hackers, and the establishment—the venture capitalists, corporate investors, and industry giants like Intel, who were now courting the company.

The dynamics of the two worlds could not have been more different.

Linux was truly a child of the Internet, communally enhanced thanks to the talent of thousands of programmers worldwide. Because of our belief in where the Internet was going, we invested significant time and resources in supporting the developers who built these tools.

The Linux-based operating systems, such as Red Hat's, were built out of a growing inventory of public tools. These tools were contributed by three groups: a large and rapidly growing team of professional corporate developers, commercial software companies, and individual programmers working in their dorm rooms and basements. But the bulk of the work was being done by the professional developers whose primary interest in these technologies was that they were also users of these tools. While this is true, the world naturally assumes that software is written by commercial companies to end up on the shelves of CompUSA and other software retailers.

But, in fact, most software is written by professionals in order to solve their organizations' internal computing needs. For example, software is developed by engineers at NASA to position radio telescopes or by insurance companies to sell more insurance. The second largest group of software programmers are the ones who contribute to open source software products simply because by doing so they get to use better products than they would have if they did not contribute. A great example of this enlightened self-interest that drives the open source movement is the graphical front-end to Linux-based operating systems called the X Window System.

In Linux, there are two levels of graphic technology at work. The foundation is the X Window System that enables the operating system to display graphics. The second is the desktop user interface. For the Linux-based operating systems, there are two desktop user interfaces to chose from, Gnome and KDE, but we'll get to that in a later chapter.

The X Window system is the graphical front end originally developed for Unix. Sun Microsystems, Hewlett Packard, IBM, and Digital (which was acquired by Compaq) all needed a graphical front end to their versions of Unix. They all recognized that by cooperating and building this tool together they could reduce their development costs and end up with a common tool that would appeal to the software application developers who wanted the versions of Unix to interoperate as much as possible.

In addition to lowering development costs and creating a mutual tool, they needed to work together simply for efficiency. Trouble would certainly arise if only one company owned the resulting code (as opposed to all of them mutually) because the others would then be beholden to the copyright holder. The group's concern was based on the fact that by being the copyright holder, an individual company could use their ownership for competitive advantage by charging high royalties to the other users of the software, or by adding features that benefited their products at the expense of their competitors. Given that their competitors were the same companies who helped them develop the technology to begin with was definitely a problem.

So they did the obvious thing and decided to work together. They agreed to publish the X Window System under an open source license. That way, they achieved their two primary goals; they reduced their individual development costs and were all able to use the same tool for their respective versions of Unix without giving up control to any one member of the X Window System development team.

Today the X Window System is maintained by X.org, the descendant of the original X Consortium. X.org includes the original members of the X development team plus new users of this technology including some Linux-based OS builders (including Red Hat).

But the public perception of the open source movement and of the Linux kernel in particular is that it was due to the work of code composers around the world, who created a masterpiece by passing bits of code.

Many believe the growth of Linux was due to the work of code composers around the world—passing bits of code between themselves like shards of a sacred score, pieces of an unfinished symphony. Far from the slick personae of the venture capital world and the polished "suits" of Fortune 500 companies, these were the offbeat Amadeuses of an unlikely digital orchestra—mostly male, many with hair to their waists, sometimes bleached blonde or DayGlo orange. They shrugged at authority, and programmed for the love of it as well as for the prestige gained from the respect of one's peers. This was an aesthetic more often observed among artists than among corporate employees. For these unlikely composers, the big reward was still in what was created as opposed to money or business deals.

The Linux kernel was the grand opus of the likes of Ted T'so, Ingo Molnar, Leonard Zubnik, Alan Cox, David Miller, and dozens of others, including—of course—Linus.

There were many "distributions," or versions, of Linux—Red Hat Linux was just one of many. The other Linux versions were products with names such as Debian, Slackware, and SuSE, monikers that sounded like they should have come from the fantasy world of Lord of the Rings.

The difference with Red Hat's product was, after years of persistence, we had managed to create the brand reliability and recognition that was now attracting mainstream corporations. Our goal had always been to become the Heinz ketchup of the Linux world—low cost, high quality, reliable, and predictable.

In fact, numerous Red Hat executives poked fun at me for my comparisons of Red Hat's brand position in the operating system market with Heinz Ketchup's brand in the food business—part of my sales pitch to investors. Yet every word was sincere.

Now Red Hat was facing the establishment—preparing for a critical pow-wow with Intel's business development team and senior vice president John Miner, head of its Enterprise Server Group.

The initial series of face-to-face meetings with Intel had commenced a couple of months earlier when I had paid a visit to the company's Oregon offices. Bruce Greer had invited me to talk about the demand Intel was getting from the scientific community. Brookhaven National Labs and Fermilab, among others, had been pushing Intel to support Linux at the microprocessor level.

A few weeks later, Wookie arrived at our offices in North Carolina. Wookie was the nickname for Intel's Tim Witham. He continued the talks about Intel's broader interest in Linux and the new opportunities it afforded.

That was followed by a strategic meeting on April 27, with Intel's Enterprise Server Group, again in Oregon. Accompanying me at that first meeting were Marc Ewing, Erik Troan, Donnie Barnes, and a dozen Intel executives and managers—nine of them present, and at least three present by phone.

Ewing, the co-founder and Chief Technical Officer of Red Hat, Inc. built the first Red Hat Linux distribution in the spare bedroom of his apartment near Duke University in North Carolina. This first Red Hat Linux distribution, called the Halloween release, was on October 31, 1994.

Troan, Red Hat's head of development and a well-regarded Linux programmer, had been with the company since June of 1995. When Ewing posted a note on the Internet looking for a developer, Troan responded.

Barnes, head of internal systems and Red Hat's official ambassador to the open source community, also had been with Red Hat since June of 1995, and had been cruising the Internet and using Linux long before he joined the company.

During the meeting, we could see that Intel had been startled by its market study which revealed that Linux represented a substantial percentage of all the operating systems Intel was shipping in the marketplace on its server microprocessors.

Intel was aware that our company was making significant inroads in corporate accounts with sophisticated users who were overseeing computer networks. These users appreciated access to the innards of the Linux system. Use of Red Hat Linux was also exploding on server computers used to host Web sites.

At the same time, Intel itself was riding an industry trend toward handling more and more computing tasks on the server rather than the desktop—a trend also fueled by the explosion of the Internet. This trend could potentially unseat Microsoft, whose power base was on the desktop.

Intel recognized that it had no strategy to deal with the surprising number of computer companies, ISPs, and customers who were using Linux—it had come out of nowhere. How would it support its customers who were using Linux-based servers? How would they support the resellers and system integrators who were selling these systems?

Intel wanted to find out why its studies showed that Red Hat had the dominant market share, and what was really driving this market. We jointly began exploring how Intel should work with Red Hat to get its own technologies deployed on Linux—which had broader strategic importance than merely participating in a new market.

Intel owned its position in the marketplace because it's among the most effective marketing organizations in the world, as is Microsoft, for that matter. Intel knew what was happening in the market before anyone else. Venture capitalists are the same way: They make their money off of knowing what's happening in the market before anyone else does.

After the first meeting, I decided I wasn't really needed. After all, I'm a sales guy, while the others were technology buffs, and Intel clearly was already sold on Linux.

In many ways, the world had come full circle.

One of the open software movement's early gurus, MIT's Richard Stallman, founded the Free Software Foundation back in 1984, frustrated that he could not fix the printer in his office. The manufacturer refused to give access to the source code that would enable Stallman to fix the bug himself.

Commercial software companies normally only shop "binaries" to their software—the 1's and 0's that the computer understands. They retain as their own intellectual property the source code that programmers might use to tailor the software to their particular needs.

When Stallman referred to free software, he explained that he meant "free" in the sense of "free speech" versus "free beer." Free software, or open source software, meant that the software came with source code and a license that allowed the user to make modifications. Purists like Stallman believed that developing software in a manner that allowed the resulting technology to be shared with others was as important as free speech. Not because it is the moral thing to do, but because a society based on freedom—free speech and free markets—simply works better than the alternative.

At Red Hat, we believed that software built under an open source model worked better and cost less to both build and maintain. In some ways, this was a throwback to what the industry was like some 30 years ago. Looking at the history of software development, it was only in 1965 that IBM ceased bundling the source code with the operating systems of their computers. In the grand scheme of things, the proprietary nature of software is a relatively recent phenomenon in the software development business.

Prior to the halt in releasing their code, IBM needed the help of all their users to build reliable operating systems. By 1965, however, the company was big enough and had a large enough programming staff that it could afford to build its operating systems without the help of the user community.

The first version of Unix was written in 1969 by Ken Thompson, a researcher at AT&T's Bell Labs. It was further developed during the 1970s by staff at AT&T's Bell Labs for an internal project. AT&T had purchased a large number of minicomputers from companies like Digital, Prime, Perkin Elmer, Wang and HP, and was having difficulty getting these computers to talk to each other because of the lack of standards between the various operating systems these computers ran. AT&T decided that it might be easier to build a common portable operating system that could be run on all these different computers, making them easier to interconnect. This project was the beginning of Unix.

At the time, AT&T was a regulated phone company, and as such, was prohibited from getting into the computer business, or any other business. In return for this restriction, the government allowed AT&T to run a regulated monopoly in long-distance phone service. When universities and research organizations asked to be allowed in on the Unix project, AT&T was pleased to send them all the source code at no cost, because it stood to benefit from the contributions these organizations could make.

The Unix source code was distributed freely throughout the 1970s, and soon became popular at universities and research labs. This limitless free distribution enabled strong computer curriculum universities, such as MIT and the University of California at Berkeley, to become significant contributors to the building of the Unix operating system.

In 1984, Judge Harold Greene broke up AT&T into the six regional baby Bells. The remaining AT&T company owned a lot of assets, including all the manufacturing capacity of the old AT&T but without the long-distance phone monopoly. Therefore, the new AT&T had to find a way to make a return on its assets. Suddenly, realizing that the copyright to Unix was a valuable asset, they began to charge the Unix users standard license fees. With this, they also began to charge their Unix development partners, including Berkeley and MIT. Needless to say, the programmers at Berkeley, MIT, and elsewhere who had contributed to the building of Unix were not pleased.

Richard Stallman's founding of the Free Software Foundation at around the same time was no coincidence. It was joined by a wide alliance of interests: people who simply did not want to pay AT&T royalties, others who just wanted continued access to the Unix source code, as well as ideologically driven people like Stallman, who had come to believe that sharing source code is similar to sharing language. Stallman believed fervently that one should not be restricted from being able to use and modify computer code any more than one should be restricted from using and modifying the English language.

Although some disagree with Stallman, even the most practical profit-oriented programmer would acknowledge that building software under an open source model results in software that simply works better.

Nevertheless, most of the successful free software projects to date had been of a technical nature—designed by engineers for their own use. It remained to be seen if the average nontechnical user would find open source software as useful.

In many ways, the success of Linux came about because it gave its users control over the great infrastructure layer that system administrators and other technical users find invaluable for building more reliable systems.

Our challenge was to use the free software model to build products that satisfied the needs of both the technical and non-technical users.

———

A month after our April meeting with Intel's server division, at a time when the talks were beginning to take a more serious tone, we brought Paul McNamara, a former IBM executive, on board to manage the emerging relationship and other new relationships that would soon evolve.

McNamara was brought in to another series of meetings that were becoming increasingly intense. Now present was Andre Turenne, an investment scout inside Intel. The company had these guys scattered among various operating divisions, keeping their eyes open for new strategic opportunities and partnerships.

A key promoter of the partnership with Red Hat inside Intel was Scott Richardson, working with John Miner in the enterprise server group. Richardson was becoming a thought leader inside of Intel, and would quickly rise to be vice president of Internet services.

Intel had sensed that there was a new dimension being formed in the marketplace—and an opportunity it didn't want to miss. We recognized that relationships with companies like Intel would help shepherd Red Hat into the mainstream marketplace.

The Internet was transforming the normal patterns of the industry, and Intel noticed that the ISP market was growing at a tremendous rate.

From its market studies, Intel recognized that Linux was very popular with the small and mid-sized ISPs. At the time, almost 20 percent of all the public Web servers were running Linux so Intel believed by understanding what was going on with Linux and by making some moves in the Linux marketplace they could potentially tap into that market and increase its penetration.

The conversation continued back and forth, and Intel began to explain to us how its investment process worked. Negotiating with Intel's business development team would serve as an eye-opening primer for any company looking to partner with an American giant. It was startling to see how this American business legend could turn on a dime to accommodate instantaneous shifts in the marketplace.

We began to engage with Intel on a variety of fronts trying to determine ways to jointly make a market impact in the Linux space. The companies engaged in co-marketing and technical discussions.

Intel soon would call in open source guru Linus Torvalds for some advice about how to be successful in this strange new environment. Intel was concerned about how they would be perceived in the marketplace. The open source community was a wildly expressive group, and Intel wanted to make sure that any moves it made in the open source arena would be received in a positive way.

Linux developers, a young and creative bunch, were predisposed to the opinion that large companies were a bad thing. Aware of this, Intel was concerned that it needed to enter the market in the right way and contribute in a positive manner.

Along with its eagerness to capture a fast-growing segment of the server market, Intel was also recognizing that Linux potentially represented the most efficient and fastest way to project new technologies into the marketplace. If Microsoft would not support its technologies, Intel could do the work for Linux itself, seeing that the source code was freely available and accessible. If it chose, Intel could also have companies like Red Hat, or others in the open source community, do the actual work to accommodate the technology.

On the morning of April 29, I was making the rounds in Silicon Valley, visiting with Netscape and Linus Torvalds and others, and I had a few hours to kill before my next meeting. I stopped at a gas station pay phone to check my messages.

The voice of Benchmark Capital's Kevin Harvey was among the messages.

I dialed Harvey's number, and to my surprise Harvey picked up the phone. "Why don't you come down for lunch with me and my partner Andy Rachleff?" Harvey asked. "We want to talk with you."

I hung up the phone and was rather stunned. On only 20 minutes' notice, I was going to lunch with two of the four general partners of the hottest venture capital firm in California.

At John Bentley's, a sleepy restaurant on Sand Hill Road in Woodside, California, the three of us talked about Red Hat's business model and the rest of the open source movement.

"We can produce better technology under the open source model," I explained. "And using the open source model we can compete with Microsoft because we're delivering a benefit to the customer that Microsoft simply can't."

Did Red Hat have plans to make part of the technology proprietary? It was a question all prospective investors had asked. The answer was, "Absolutely not." We had always been committed to shipping all of our source code under an open source license. I explained the three strategic benefits publishing all our code under open source licenses gave us. We had no interest in a proprietary play.

Harvey pointed out that he was intrigued with the open source movement and was amazed that it seemed to already have such organic momentum.

As the lunch was nearing an end, I was expecting the response from Benchmark that I'd come to expect from experience with other venture capitalists I'd spoken with: Don't call us, we'll call you.

As we got up from the lunch table, Harvey said, "We're very interested. We want you to come talk to the rest of our partners in a couple of weeks."

———

By June 1998, the Intel talks had gotten rather intense.

The email message McNamara sent on Friday, June 26, to Red Hat management indicated that an investment deal was imminent. McNamara had spoken with Intel's Alan Holtzman and Turenne, who acknowledged that Intel preferred to make an equity investment in its business partners, although it was not absolutely necessary.

We had not yet informed Intel that we had been approached by a world class venture capitalist. "I hedged a bit but told them that we were talking to a few different people," McNamara wrote in his email. He didn't want to show his hand as he didn't know what type of investment deal might be struck with Benchmark Capital and Kevin Harvey.

Intel picked up on this. McNamara wrote in his email, "They indicated that they liked to do investment deals with VCs where the VC took the lead and Intel just supplied money in the deal. They asked if we were talking to any top-tier VCs. I told them we were talking to Benchmark. They were very happy about this."

The range of Intel's typical investment in small companies was $2 to $5 million. Holtzman proposed a meeting face to face the following Thursday.

———

Andy Grove's lieutenants were in a state of disbelief.

It was early July, and Red Hat executives traveled once more to Intel's Oregon offices. We all congregated in a conference room, and the meeting had been going on for about an hour when the mood shifted. Along with Paul McNamara and the others, I was facing Andre Turenne, Scott Richardson, Alan Holtzman, and their colleagues.

As I gave my presentation, Turenne kept swiveling impatiently in his chair. "Bob, don't you have any charts?" he asked.

"No, we don't have any charts," I replied, and continued with my pitch. I explained that Red Hat doesn't own any of its software, and did not have any intellectual property rights like a proprietary software company does. Instead, our focus was convenience and relationship.

Ordinarily when small companies go before the microprocessor giant, they put on slick, formal presentations based on traditional business models in the software business that they know investors will be interested in. In our case, our business model was so revolutionary and different, we didn't have a formal presentation. After all, we were talking about making money selling free software. Our goal was to have Intel come away with the understanding that this was an entirely new model that would be shaping the patterns of the software industry for the next ten to fifteen years.

As I continued, Turenne kept swiveling nervously. He was a no-nonsense guy who viewed the world in numbers.

"We're talking about an operating system model where we can not exert any proprietary control over our customers or partners," I said. "We have to earn our customers business every day, and this has profound advantages for both the customer and the other participants and partners in terms of their whole view of the operating system."

Intel had courted us for weeks, but now during the final pitch, we seemed to have lost our audience. The Intel guys were all on the verge of nodding off, according to Paul McNamara, who was paying more close attention to our listeners.

Finally Turenne, almost beside himself, was on his feet. "Bob, I just don't understand. I just don't think this is an investable model!"

Red Hat had heard this many times before. I replied, "Now wait Andre, we're only halfway into it." Turenne sat back down.

Scott Richardson began piping up, reinforcing my message with some of the things he was seeing with customers. He shared with Turenne what Intel had discovered with respect to ISPs and their use of Linux. Richardson was intent on eroding his colleague's skepticism. He began to insist that this was an important model to Intel, and Turenne began to pay more attention.

As Paul McNamara would later describe it, by the end of the meeting, we had made a group of converts out of our skeptical friends at Intel.

By mid July, simultaneous talks with both Intel and venture capitalist Benchmark were far along.

Seeing that we are an East Coast company, Kevin Harvey urged us to bring in another VC to this round of funding—the top East Coast firm Greylock Management—one of the founding venture capital companies in America. Over the years, Greylock had funded more than 75 software companies.

In July, while heading for a beach holiday in North Carolina, a two-hour drive to the coast, I reached Greylock partner Bill Kaiser on my cell phone. Although the call was interrupted regularly with lapses in the phone connection, we managed to talk for almost an hour about our potential relationship. For only the second time, I found myself talking to a venture capitalist who was not immediately turned off by the idea of giving away our source code.

Shortly after, Ewing and I flew to Boston for a face-to-face meeting with Kaiser. We discovered that Kaiser was fond of using an unconventional sales technique: He insisted that Red Hat was doing really well and he didn't understand why the company needed Greylock. This put us in a position of extolling the virtues of working with Greylock. The two sides started selling each other's positions to each other. Kaiser was arguing why Red Hat shouldn't work with Greylock, and Red Hat was telling Greylock why working with Greylock would be the best thing since sliced bread.

In the course of the discussions, we also acknowledged that, at this point in time, we had a relatively thin management team and that our market opportunity was massive. To get to the next level, we would need people on board who have a vested interest in the long term, and who would introduce us to the caliber of executive candidates we might have difficulty attracting on our own. It was a role Greylock could provide.

We later became great advocates for the benefits of working with VCs. We reaped decades of experience from the counsel provided by both Greylock and Benchmark.

The interesting thing about Bill Kaiser was that he had seen the impact of an open systems approach in the early days of the industry. Kaiser would soon become a board member. He seemed a particularly good fit for Red Hat as he had come out of a sales environment with Hewlett-Packard and Apollo computer. One of the things that convinced us that Kaiser was the right guy for a board position was his business experience with Apollo.

When Kaiser was with Apollo, he watched the company, within a 36-month time frame, go from $12 million in revenue to $300 million in revenue. Ironically, while this financial growth was happening, Apollo had gone from number one in its industry to number two. Kaiser considered his experience with Apollo to have been a failure despite that phenomenal growth rate, because of its loss of market share.

Red Hat was in a stage that would benefit from Kaiser's experience. We were number one in our industry and on track to do $10- to $11-million worth of business. We needed management that could help us avoid the mistakes that would possibly be the right thing for shareholders in the short term but the wrong thing for the industry in the long term.

Interestingly, Apollo was Sun's big competitor in its early days. When Apollo slid to number two, it was Sun, moving up from the number two spot, that had taken over the lead. The turning point, ironically, was based on open systems versus proprietary systems. Apollo had a proprietary view of network-connected workstations, whereas Sun had a Unix-based, open systems view.

Kaiser understood our need to drive our market very quickly, as that was our only defensible position. We needed to be the guys who grew the market the fastest.

On the ferry ride back from Greylock's offices to Boston's Logan airport, Ewing and I both agreed we should get two venture capitalists for the price of one. Both Greylock and Benchmark would be in on the next investment round.

All of us at Red Hat recognized the weight of taking on an unbelievable challenge: We were confronting the twentieth century's best marketing organization—Microsoft—owner of an operating system standard and a monopoly in the marketplace.

Next, we knew we had to build a management team and an organization capable of looking after our customers.

Greylock would eventually help recruit Red Hat president Matthew Szulik.

Meanwhile, at Intel, Richardson and Turenne took the deal forward for review to the Intel senior VP responsible for investments. We were informed that the terms of a deal would be laid out and a decision would be made.

Scott Richardson and his boss John Miner would be the official "sponsors" of the deal inside Intel, promoting to their bosses the importance of the investment to Intel.

A few weeks later, we were informed by phone the deal was a "go." The formal investment round began to be structured.

By the end of July, Benchmark and Greylock were urging Red Hat to follow the standard industry practice of allowing them to invest first, and then later—and at a higher price—allow corporate investors in.

Venture capitalists often hope to double or triple a startup's valuation from one financing round to the next. They assumed that Intel would not come in the next round, at a higher price.

While July unfurled its heat waves over the North Carolina landscape, Paul McNamara made a phone call to Andre Turenne at Intel to inform him of the company's plans.

"We want to do this deal with you guys, but we don't want to do it until November," McNamara said.

Dead silence.

Then from Turenne, "What's going on?"

McNamara explained. "We have some prior commitments about funding rounds and..."

Turenne came unglued.

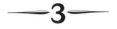

—3—

Funding A Revolution

"During the past year, Linux has risen to the forefront among the relatively unknown products that can substitute for the Windows software program."

—*The Wall Street Journal*

PAUL MCNAMARA WAS HOLDING THE PHONE receiver six inches from his ear. Andre Turenne was shouting, and McNamara could hear him pounding on the table.

"I know what these guys are trying to do!" Turenne shouted. "They're trying to cut us out of the round so they can come back to us with a higher valuation. We're not going to go for it! I've seen venture capitalists do this before....!"

McNamara got off the phone. That was an interesting call, he thought, and went to find me.

"Andre is really upset," McNamara said.

I picked up the phone and dialed Turenne's office. McNamara sat by. Soon, I was holding the receiver six inches away from my ear. Turenne was still fuming; he was beside himself. He wanted in, and would not take "no" for an answer. He would not wait for a later round.

We went back to talk to our venture capital partners.

We had a situation where everyone wanted to throw money at us, but on their own terms. No one would accept that we couldn't take their money if they were going to insist on terms and conditions that conflicted with those proposed by the other investors.

———

In the meantime, Netscape was waiting in the wings.

Since early in the year, dramatic developments were brewing at the company, which had years earlier catalyzed Microsoft's all-out attack on the browser market.

For some time, Netscape had been an avid supporter of Linux, and had been carefully following the success of Red Hat. The proliferation of Linux in 1998 was driven by a number of events, including Netscape's surprise announcement a few months earlier of its Mozilla project, which would open up the source code to its browser technology. Since 1995 Netscape had offered a binary-only version of its browser for Linux. The Mozilla announcement meant that the open source software developers could contribute to the development of the Netscape browsers.

With its Mozilla announcement, Netscape essentially validated the open source model. Open source guru Eric Raymond referred to Netscape's move as "the shot heard round the world." Indeed, industry insiders viewed it as one of the seminal events of 1998.

On April 28, 1998, the day before my first meeting with Benchmark's Kevin Harvey, I had met once again with Netscape executives to investigate areas of joint product engineering interest. Present were Marc Andreessen; John Paul, Netscape's senior vice president for server engineering; and three others within Netscape. Andreessen was a soft spoken engineer's engineer, who reminded me of our Marc Ewing. We also talked with Ben Horowitz, an effective technology manager who understood the opportunities that open source and Red Hat represented to Netscape.

Netscape's primary problem was always one of market position: Its technology required Microsoft technology to work. The lion's share of browsers shipped by Netscape ran on Windows.

When Microsoft added browser functionality directly to the Windows operating system, it materially damaged Netscape's browser market share. This new development in the Windows OS also damaged the demand for Netscape's Server products because most of the browsers in use were from Microsoft and hence "tuned" for Microsoft servers. To make matters worse, Microsoft also managed to get many Web sites to include its "best viewed with Internet Explorer" logo, further damaging market acceptance of Netscape's software.

Nevertheless, any company that could go from start-up to being sold for $10 billion (the final value paid by AOL by the time the deal closed) in less than 5 years, has to be considered a huge success.

Netscape's chief technology officer Eric Hahn was also a big fan and in regular contact with Red Hat, and in discussions about a technical collaboration between the two companies.

Like other industry watchers, Netscape's perceptions of Red Hat were supported by a market study by International Data Corp. (IDC), which showed that Red Hat had 56 percent of the total market share.

By that time, it was no secret that Red Hat was in talks with both Intel and venture capital firms, and was headed for another investment round. The idea of an investment on the part of Netscape quickly came up, and Netscape was eager for this to happen, despite the fact that it was making few investments in outside companies at the time. Quincy Smith, director of mergers and acquisitions at Netscape, and Horowitz, would keep in constant touch with McNamara and others, waiting for the dust to settle in the Intel negotiations.

Smith was a financial executive at Netscape, who reported to CFO Peter Curry. (He would later leave to join a venture capital firm.) Red Hat's McNamara met with Smith to explain the details of the potential investment round the company was putting together with the other investors.

During the entire investment proceedings Netscape never wavered. As the negotiations continued on with the VC's and Intel, Netscape's Smith repeated, "Just send us the documents."

———

History repeats itself and this was a revolution not unlike others.

As we headed toward the most important funding round, I would explain the evolution of Red Hat's business for would-be investors as if describing a historical event in the creation of the free world. Our belief that we would succeed, despite the odds of competing in our current market, was driven by the philosophy that all revolutions succeed once enough people are empowered with enough information to understand the benefits the new ideas offered over the old ones.

Many years ago, New England merchants and bankers had come forward to fund the American revolution. In effect, Intel, Netscape, Benchmark, and Greylock were acting like those merchants, helping to ensure the success of the open source movement.

As a former history major, I am always tempted to compare the open source movement to other great uprisings in the history of the world and this was no exception.

During prior periods in history, mankind organized itself into feudal systems in which a few educated people took responsibility of managing society for everyone. The average person was very much dependent on the noble classes to look after his best interests: to set the laws and to determine whether to wage war, and so on. In the late 18th century, a series of revolutions occurred worldwide because the average individual had become better educated. As education became more widespread, a larger group of people were capable of contributing to the direction of society.

In the software business, companies built software behind closed doors and kept control of the software tools, and the users of that software, by not allowing users access to the information—source code—that users would need to fix or improve the software. This resulted in a feudal relationship between the software users and their suppliers. Open source offers the user the opportunity to break out of the tyrannical control that binary-only software suppliers are able to exercise over their customers.

Prior to the American revolution, taxes and laws were largely handed down from the British king and the British parliament to the American population. The American population recognized this wasn't necessarily in their best interest: They felt that they had a contribution to make and wanted it to be reflected in their laws.

What was interesting about the American revolution was that there were groups of individuals who were the leaders with innovative ideas. They were the Patrick Henrys who said, "Give me liberty or give me death." The collective contributions of the businesses in the communities, however, are what paid for the supplies for George Washington's army—the cannons, uniforms, muskets, and any other supplies they needed.

The revolution was driven by both the individuals and the merchant class. Both groups recognized an economic system was needed that worked on behalf of all the participants in a society and not just on behalf of the elite.

Red Hat and its would-be investors were acting like those New England merchants—supporting rebel programmers so they could continue their efforts, investing R&D money to deliver new technology to the movement.

It was Red Hat's commitment to this fundamental shift in the software business that enabled us to drive the marketplace. We were delivering more of a unique benefit than our competitors who appeared to be trying to succeed based on their faith that Linux was simply a better technology than Microsoft's. But the industry was littered with the corpses of companies who were delivering better technology. Being better did not mean you would win in an arena where one company was leveraging its market power.

Delivering unique benefits to your customers is critical in any market if you hope to make inroads against a dominant player like

Microsoft. Our unique benefit was that we were giving control of the product to the user instead of retaining control over our users. If you move into an industry playing by its existing rules, you'll just become another player. You won't revolutionize that industry unless you change the paradigm. We were also offering a solution at a dramatically lower cost, attacking an overpriced market segment.

It is interesting to note that few would have believed it if, in 1992, they'd been told that soon a cooperatively built group of integrated networks, with no one in charge and no one company in control, would be the foundation of exploding new businesses all over the world. That network, of course, is the Internet, and it is currently being embraced by the world. We have seen and experienced the benefits of a network built on open standards that don't require a controlling authority. Instead of one sole authoritative person or company, the community of users are the authority.

The same practice holds true for the development of Linux. The Linux programming community, engineers working for large and small organizations, as well as independent programmers, is continually looking to participate in the enhancement of the product by sharing their knowledge and constructively critiquing each other's work. They communicate back and forth in an effort to enhance Linux. Everyone is in it together.

───────

By the end of summer, a deal was struck that included everyone: Intel, Netscape, Greylock, and Benchmark. In the end, Intel ended up accepting a slightly smaller investment than it would have preferred but were able to get in this round at a better valuation.

Some last minute wrangling went on before Intel began drawing up the papers. In the meantime, it sent out some of its financial sleuths to do some final work.

Lila Partridge, Intel's senior treasury manager for strategic investments and acquisitions, arrived at Red Hat's North Carolina office, along with her colleague Tammy Hutchinson. Together, they put us through our paces, grilling Paul McNamara and other executives about the company's business model.

During this particular meeting, while I was eloquently sharing my Heinz ketchup analogy with Partridge (a very sophisticated money manager), I noticed that she too, like the other Intel executives, looked quite bored. Selling free software is a business model finance people have a hard time getting their minds around. Partridge interrupted, pointing out defects in my analogy and going into detail about the price of tomato futures and how this might affect the cost and profitability of ketchup. Paul McNamara found this amusing, and all present decided to forget about analogies and stick to the facts. After a day of due diligence, Red Hat had passed the Partridge test and the deal was close to completion.

It was now September 1998, still the same year this investment opportunity came to our door, and ISPCON, an industry show for Internet Service Providers, was in full swing. Paul McNamara and Marc Ewing stood in line waiting for their badges, and still had not received word if the deal was final. We were planning to announce at the conference that we had four new investors.

But somehow the story had already leaked, and the press was running wild with it—speculating that it represented a split between Intel and Microsoft, and an end to the Microsoft/Intel duopoly.

But all the paperwork still had not been signed, and we were trying to track down shareholders all over the globe, who had to sign off on the deal. We were still wrangling over last-minute details with Netscape and Intel.

McNamara was wondering if the announcement would have to be pulled, as he had not yet received the call that the deal was done. It's not unheard of in such deals that, even after all the paperwork is signed, the deal can be called off. Nothing was certain until the money was actually wired into Red Hat's account.

The lines were growing longer, and the conference crowd was pouring in. Then McNamara's cell phone rang. It was David Shumanfang, Red Hat's chief counsel, informing him that the deal was done.

McNamara pressed the "end" button on his cell phone, and turned to Ewing grinning. The two shook hands.

On September 28th, 1998, Red Hat announced that it had closed an investment round with two industry giants, Intel and Netscape, and with two of the world's leading venture capital firms, Benchmark Capital and Greylock Management.

The buzz on Wall Street and in the media could not have been anticipated.

The Wall Street Journal called the announcement "a potentially significant endorsement for an upstart challenger to Microsoft Corp.'s dominance in operating-system software."

Further analyzing the deal, the conservative paper stated, "During the past year, Linux has risen to the forefront among the relatively unknown products that can substitute for the Windows software program."

It acknowledged that Linux's popularity was in part due to the fact that its source code—the underlying blueprint for the system—is freely available over the Internet.

Shortly after the announcement, *The Economist* blared the news worldwide, stating, "Mr. Gates may feel a little queasy about the Red Hat alliance for another reason. It is the first time that Intel has directly invested in a company that markets an alternative to Windows."

Behind the scenes, Microsoft went ballistic after Intel announced its investment in Red Hat. We heard later that many Intel executives had taken angry calls that weekend from their counterparts at Microsoft. Bill Gates would soon grill Andy Grove about his decision to support Linux. Microsoft seemed careful not to make any overt threats. The Justice Department was watching closely.

Nevertheless, Microsoft was in the process of deploying a Linux attack team, a group of engineers and marketers, whose focus was to counter the growing use of Linux on the part of its customers. The team's mission was to convince potential corporate users that Linux was not ready for prime time.

The significance of closing this round with Intel and Netscape was that it made Linux-based operating systems safe for the major application vendors, including Oracle, Corel, and Computer Associates. They would now be willing to sell their applications to their customers running on Red Hat Linux.

But back in Silicon Valley, Kevin Harvey had already spoken to Michael Dell, the chairman and CEO of Dell Computer Corporation, and planted an idea.

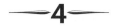

Dominoes

"The computer industry is so competitive, people really have a hard time getting used to the notion that maybe sometimes you can agree to be friends."

—Linus Torvalds

A PARADE OF OTHER INDUSTRY GIANTS would soon line up to become part of the open source uprising.

In the meantime, we were getting a whirlwind education while rethinking our business plan on the fly. Prior to the second round of funding, in early February 1998, Red Hat Linux engineer Michael Johnson sent an email message to everyone at the company: Red Hat had once again won the Infoworld product of the year award. But even in the face of such accolades, the company recognized it had a problem.

As of early 1998, Red Hat Linux was being recognized as having an operating system that was as good or better than anything any of the proprietary operating system vendors could offer, but the commercial customers were not buying it. Instead, they were choosing dramatically more expensive alternatives from Microsoft, IBM, and Sun Microsystems.

The reason was almost exclusively due to the perceived safety in buying server operating system technology from multibillion-dollar organizations. Even if Red Hat doubled—or even quadrupled—in size overnight, it would still be perceived as being an "unsafe" choice when compared to the competition simply due to the fact that we weren't as large and we weren't bringing in as much revenue.

How to solve this?

If the only way to be considered a reliable supplier of server operating system technology was to be a billion-dollar company, we could always do the next best thing: Partner with the industry's leading suppliers that might benefit from having alternative operating system suppliers.

Red Hat needed to continue on the path it had begun when it entered into partnerships with Netscape and Intel. Our management made a list of organizations to go after. A major hardware supplier and a major enterprise software supplier would be desirable.

Intel had been at the top of the hardware supplier list: It represented the common denominator because it built the chips that ran the other suppliers' computers. Netscape had been at the top of the software suppliers' list. Even though it wasn't the largest, it was the most visible.

Now we would go after other market leaders. In the beginning, we had no idea where to start. None of our founding executives had ever sold anything worth more than a small minicomputer, and while we had been recruiting a more experienced team, we understand that we were attempting to sell the industry's most aggressive companies on a bizarre notion. Once again, they were being asked to invest large amounts of money in a very small software company whose business plan required that it give away the source code to all the software it developed.

Soon we were in the midst of our next round of financing, what we called the "C" round, and lining up investments from IBM, Compaq, Dell, Novell, Oracle, and SAP.

What was most surprising was how easy it was to get these industry giants interested, and the subsequent need to stand our ground in the face of tough negotiating sessions with executives at these multibillion dollar corporations. We often had to stare down executives at these companies on important issues just to get these deals closed.

Normally when a company with a staff of 30,000 people and multi-billion dollars in revenues decides to invest in a 75-person, $10 million-a-year business, it gets to call all the shots. Often, companies will insist on having either a board seat or board observer status, and rights of first refusal on any subsequent investment rounds. They would demand that their investment have a higher security ranking in the event of bankruptcy than the existing shareholders, and similar benefits.

In our case, with six new investors and five existing institutional investors (including Batten), we did not have the ability to offer any special provisions. Some of our investors protested wildly, insisting that they "always" received such benefits.

All of the companies that were eager to invest in our Linux-based business were aggressive marketing organizations who did not want to see their competitors gain an advantage they did not have. They also had achieved their successes by being customer-oriented and were highly attuned to the customer interest in Linux and other open source software tools.

By the time we contacted all of them, we had additional factors working for us: introductions by people they respected (either directly or indirectly through Bill Kaiser or Kevin Harvey); market research backing up our business (as mentioned previously, IDC had estimated our market share at 56 percent of all Linux products sold worldwide, compared to 8 percent for our nearest competitor); and the fact that customers were asking them for Linux-based products, and Red Hat Linux in particular.

When it came down to agreeing on the specifics of the investment round, we could not afford to listen to the demands of these companies too closely, as each had its own set of demands. There was no way we could give in to one without offering the same conditions to the others. And these demands frequently came from our existing shareholders as well, each of whom could have scuttled the whole investment round by insisting on protections that might not have been acceptable to the new investors or to the other existing investors.

While Benchmark, Greylock, Frank Batten Jr., Intel, and Netscape were a help to us in attracting the interest of these new investors in our C round, they became more of the problem in the effort to close that round.

Management at Red Hat, led by Matthew Szulik, and including Paul McNamara, Manoj George, and Dave Shumanfang in particular, along with Bill Shnoor and Greg Griner of our law firm Testa Hurwitz and Tibault in Boston, did a brilliant job of negotiating the minefield that the conflicting demands of these six new multibillion-dollar investors represented.

On a regular basis we had to call executives at Oracle, Novell, Compaq, and the others and explain that if they really required clause "X" (whatever that was) into the final documents, we would be really sorry to lose them from this investment round. Although Red Hat would not be able to meet their condition, perhaps we would be able to meet that condition in a future round and bring them into Red Hat at that time.

Of course, in each case, the investor would abandon its demand for fear of being left out of an opportunity that was going to be important to its success in the open source software marketplace.

After each of these calls, our chief counsel, Dave Shumanfang, and I would just sit down together, shake our heads, and chuckle over the thought that we—a small team based in the tobacco fields of North Carolina—had just stared down another industry giant.

It seemed very surreal to us—while at the same time being a very exciting adventure.

———————

When starting to work with IBM Corp., we found ourselves in a dance that reminded us of the strategic wrangling in the early days of the PC market, when IBM first formed a partnership with Microsoft for the DOS operating system. While our situation was much different, it again involved a David partnering with a Goliath. In those early days, Microsoft had managed to gain control of the DOS operating system because of a mistake on IBM's part that allowed Microsoft to collect all royalties for the operating system. Since that time, IBM became paranoid of any little company getting the upper hand, especially in the strategic area of operating systems.

The first meetings started in October 1998, with various marketing managers at IBM, and proceeded slowly. The possibilities were being slowly and carefully evaluated.

Soon, David Sink brought in his group from IBM's software organization, and Nancy Fagan, vice president of IBM's e-business unit, began to participate. There was interest in collaborating in the server business in the area of support and co-marketing.

But things moved at a snail's pace with IBM, as McNamara knew, being a former IBM executive. Nothing got nailed down at these meetings. After scores of additional meetings and conference calls, a meeting was held in February 1999, led by IBM's vice president of network software Al Zoller.

IBM was studying all the market indicators that showed that Linux was taking off. In a broader context, IBM had been watching the open source movement closely and had actually already completed a deal with the Apache group in late 1998. (Apache is used by more than half of all Web sites on the Internet, and IBM chose it to be the foundation of its Web commerce software.) Finally, when the time was right, we offered IBM the opportunity to become part of our C round of funding.

Red Hat executives drove down the street to IBM's big North Carolina facility in RTP to meet with Bob Dies, a vice president in IBM's personal systems group. Dies met with McNamara and Billy Marshall, another IBM veteran and Red Hat manager working with McNamara. In the meeting it was decided that we should put together a memorandum of understanding. Zoller would become the sponsor within IBM for the investment.

At one point in the meeting, Dies made a comment that echoed of IBM's paranoia about its past track record in the PC operating systems space.

"You need to understand we can just come in and take this market from you," he said, causing some puzzlement on the part of McNamara. After all, we are in a new business based on collaboration more than aggression. Dies added, "But we don't want to do that. It makes more sense to do a deal with you."

The investment idea was brought to the most senior management at IBM and was approved. By March 1999, we signed a letter of intent.

Of course, long before, we already had considered that IBM—or any other manufacturer, for that matter—could create its own Linux-based operating system. For example, IBM could create "IBM Linux." When we analyzed that, we decided there was really no benefit to IBM doing that. We were talking about free software, and it has been difficult enough for IBM and others to enter the operating system market with proprietary offerings such as OS/2. It was clear that IBM would have better success using the same Linux-based operating system as everyone else did.

Moreover, Red Hat does not exert any proprietary control over its partners or customers, so there would be no strategic advantage for IBM to do an IBM Linux.

IBM, being the giant that it is, also had some legal concerns.

———⟡———

Despite the deal having been approved, announced to the press, and a letter of intent signed, by June 1999 Red Hat was still wrangling with

IBM and negotiating the final contract. The contract negotiations had been brutal, with every minute point requiring hours and hours of talks with them.

Considering its history, perhaps IBM's caution in negotiating supply and support contracts with us was understandable. After all, IBM had been doing battle in the operating system market for some 20 years going back to the ill-fated deal with Microsoft in 1981. Most people who look at that deal agree that IBM gave too much control to Microsoft. On the hardware side, however, IBM had done its deals properly, creating an open standard for personal computers so customers could go to Compaq or Dell or any number of others and get the same kind of hardware.

Microsoft, on the other hand, got complete control over the operating system, and over the past 20 years IBM has tried unsuccessfully to win that back.

Throughout the remaining negotiations, we had our defenses up in case IBM did not share a common interest with us. Its mistrust was fueling our mistrust. The negotiations continued on in a difficult manner, with long wrangling sessions that did not result in any conclusions.

Finally we threw up our hands. The breaking point was reached when executives at IBM made a totally unreasonable request. They wanted us to indemnify IBM, one of the world's largest corporations, in the unlikely case of there being a patent infringement suit. We walked away from the table.

Four weeks later, IBM reconsidered, and everyone came back to the table. IBM's representatives were ready to take another approach to the deal. They no longer insisted on us indemnifying the company.

Red Hat president Matthew Szulik and IBM's Zoller got back on the phone and went through the remaining concerns once more. Zoller assured us that IBM had Red Hat's interest in mind and to prove that, it reworked some of the language it had previously insisted upon.

IBM has good reason now to be cautious. Should it continue to do battle over the next 20 years, spending billions in the operating system market promoting its own proprietary operating systems and still not have an assured outcome? Or it could get behind the growing success of Linux-based operating systems and help ensure customers once again have a choice over which operating system they use.

For this reason, participating in the Linux market was a top priority for IBM. All of the major computer makers, for that matter, saw Linux as a small beginning in loosening Microsoft's grip, in addition to it being a technically superior product that gave control back to customers.

The first signs of interest we got from Dell Computer came during our announcement at the ISPCON trade show, where we told the world of the Netscape/Intel investment. Paul McNamara had bumped into Dell's Jack Steeg on the floor of the exhibit hall. At the time, Steeg served as Dell's director of strategic alliances, and mentioned his interest in a collaboration with Red Hat. The two exchanged business cards.

Kevin Harvey, from Benchmark Capital, had taken a board seat with Red Hat, and also had a business relationship with Michael Dell. Harvey and Dell exchanged email about Dell's interest in Linux. It was not lost on chairman Dell that Harvey had invested in Red Hat; now Dell's competitors were lining up to invest.

Soon after, Michael Dell and I began an email correspondence. He dispatched their senior VP Mike Lambert to develop a collaboration with Red Hat.

McNamara discussed the partnership possibilities with Lambert, and took him through Red Hat's view of the Linux marketplace. He was surprised by some of the numbers we were talking about, and in particular some of the studies released by the IDC that showed 17.2 percent of all 1998 server shipments were Linux-based.

Laying the groundwork for a collaboration, we had a series of negotiations with Dell Computer Corp. to try and structure a deal. We decided Red Hat Linux would be a participant in the Dell Plus program, where a customer could call and order a configuration with Red Hat installed. That evolved into a more substantive agreement in which Dell would preinstall our operating system on its machines. McNamara had a meeting with Michael Dell in Austin, Texas, around March 1999 and discussed Linux and the industry in depth, primarily from what Dell was seeing from customer demand.

In his office, Dell quizzed McNamara about what the market was looking like. He noted that Dell had a section on its Web site where users could search for answers to their hardware and software questions. According to Dell, Linux was the number-two word popping up on that site.

Because of its direct business model, Dell pointed out that the company was an excellent partner for Red Hat because it gets such direct and immediate feedback from customers.

———▸◂———

Most computer makers don't install server operating systems on server computers because it is such a difficult process. Because IBM, Compaq, and HP all sell predominantly through the reseller channel, the reseller, and not the computer manufacturer, is relied upon to load the server software on the machine and administer the license.

With Linux, of course, that's not necessarily the case. We have a potential opportunity to have computer makers preinstall the Linux system on their server machines, but it will require changing the patterns of the industry. This will take a little longer to do.

Selling Linux is such a radical departure for the existing business models of the industry that IBM and other computer makers are still studying how to set up this new business. It's still evolving. Computer makers don't want to limit their freedom of action in the future, so they're being very cautious.

Dell had been invited into our C investment round at a very early point, and showed what we felt was a strong interest. However, we received an email back from Michael Dell that led us to believe there wasn't a strong interest after all. So we went off and constructed the deal with everyone else—Compaq, IBM, Oracle, SAP, Novell—but when we were very close to announcing the deal, at the last minute Dell came back and said "we need to be in"—and would not accept no for an answer.

Currently, the key component of our relationship with Dell is that Red Hat Linux participates in the Dell Plus program. This program allows customers of Dell Computers to call and order a new computer preinstalled and configured with Red Hat Linux.

Dell has also devoted a special Web page to Linux machines and Linux software, with a link to Dell's Gigabuys, an online store for software and computer peripherals.

McNamara and Michael Dell had discussed whether Linux would eventually make an impact in the desktop operating system market. Over time, desktop machines are changing from being office suite-centric to being more browser-centric. As more and more computing tasks are becoming Internet-based, it's no longer as necessary to have all the applications (such as Microsoft Office, Word, Excel, or other third-party products) running on the desktop machine: many will be running over the Internet.

Dell agreed with that view, which made Linux a choice for things like browser appliances. A browser appliance is a low-priced, out-of-the-box machine that comes with a rich-featured browser for the primary purpose of accessing the Internet. In the near future, there will be an exploding market for such low-priced machines.

Others have dreamed up this concept before, but were ahead of their time. For example, more than ten years ago, Minitel in France had a low-cost $300 device that allowed users to create text-based email. Currently, browser appliances take that concept to a whole new level. Users can buy a low-cost appliance and plug into the Internet. Their primary purpose is for navigating the Web.

Tasks that used to be done on a desktop computer are now being done over the Internet. Linux is a great choice for these types of applications because it is low in cost, highly configurable, and very stable, which in turn keeps support requirements very low.

Some in the computing world at the moment do not seem to be aware of this opportunity, and feel that Linux has a long way to go before it is used on low-end computers by a mass audience. And rightly so—if you view the desktop computer in its current paradigm, we would have to do a lot to compete in that broad marketplace.

For instance, we'd have to get all the thousands of popular desktop applications and programs available for Linux. Currently, the applications found in CompUSA and other retail outlets are primarily developed for Wintel (Windows on an Intel machine) or Apple's Macintosh platform. However, when people are using their computers primarily as Internet appliances, the whole notion of a desktop machine changes.

In my browser, I can create email and other kinds of Web-based documents. I can even do my taxes. Now think one step beyond that to where the set-top box on your TV is a Linux machine running a browser. The functions of a TV and computer now start to be merged with the Linux technology. Just now, the idea of such products is starting to take shape.

It is too early to say which manufacturers may use Linux as the operating system on such machines, but Linux is certainly well suited for such devices.

Separately, Linus Torvalds himself has been in secret talks with manufacturers about the use of Linux on such devices.

Such devices envisioned by Dell and others would provide easy access in the home, and might link to third-generation cellular mobile phone networks or high-speed cable modem and digital subscriber loops.

Michael Dell continued to discuss the changing paradigms for desktop computing with Red Hat. For example, he talked about how users could take photographs and send them to be developed and then pick them up on the developer's FTP site as digital photos that can be stored on a computer. The Internet is changing all the patterns of how people do things in their daily lives.

Even though the handheld computer market is small now (100 million PCs were sold last year, compared to only 400,000 Windows CE and 1.2 million Palm Pilot handheld machines), Dell chief technology officer Eric Harslem sees the potential market as enormous. After all, there are 6 billion people on the planet, and the Web appliance for $100, featuring $10-a-month Internet access, would be attractive to almost everyone.

As can be expected, the public is approaching these new computing devices with caution, but eventually we will see this market explode. This caution is typical with new technologies. For example, early forays into the handheld computer market were disasters for some companies, because the market was not ready for these products and the business models had not been refined.

When we started speaking with Compaq, we found that our negotiations were complicated because the Digital Equipment part of the company had a different view of the market from the Houston-based part of the company that sold Intel-based computers.

We could move more computers that contained the Alpha microprocessor, since Red Hat has a version of Linux for this chip. However, on the Houston side, they were seeing demand from customers for Intel-based boxes and they simply wanted to just fill this need and pump out the volume.

To add to the confusion, the investment track and the collaboration side of the deal were two distinctly different developments.

Our relationship with Compaq goes back three years. John Hall, the famous "maddog" Hall, was the chief person at Compaq that was involved in the relationship at the time. (He would later leave and serve as one of the gurus of the open source movement, as head of Linux International.)

For a long time, Digital Equipment was reluctant to be vocal about its Linux strategy. More recently, however, it has seen the increase in market demand, and thus Compaq, its Houston-based parent, has become more aggressive.

It was Bob Fernander, a Compaq VP for the small to medium business unit, who was eager to get into the Linux arena, and drove the activity on that side. On the Digital side, Tim Yeaton was the promoter. Compaq saw Linux as a way to increase sales of its Alpha microprocessor.

We had been building Red Hat Linux for Digital's Alpha processors since 1996. Maddog, who had become a great friend of many of us at Red Hat, convinced us that with Digital's support, an Alpha version of Red Hat would become a great business opportunity. But despite Herculean efforts by maddog to convince Digital management to devote resources to marketing Linux-based products, nothing happened until Compaq bought Digital in early 1998. Compaq management, being a much more aggressive marketing, very quickly began to recognize the potential of marketing Linux on their Alpha computer workstations and servers.

In 1999, with intense interest in the operating system, Compaq began offering Linux on its computers about the same time that IBM, Hewlett-Packard, and Dell moved to embrace it.

Red Hat has been selling its Alpha version of Linux since 1995, along with Red Hat Package Manager (RPM), files that make it easier for Linux users to update their software with a minimum amount of technical knowledge. Compaq was particularly interested in increasing Red Hat sales of Alpha Linux and in return increasing sales of its microprocessor. It was also encouraging software vendors to translate its proprietary programs to Alpha Linux.

Clearly, Compaq executives recognized that Linux would provide the company with access to new markets for its Alpha chips. First, it was targeting the high-performance technical computing market. In such markets, Alpha computers running Linux were tied together to form a low-budget supercomputer such as Los Alamos National Laboratory's 140-processor Avalon computer. This technique, known as "Beowulf," was pioneered at NASA's Goddard Space Flight Center, and Red Hat distributes Beowulf software in its Extreme Linux product.

Compaq was next targeting the Internet Service Provider market because it believed its Alpha machines running Linux offer higher performance to these companies. In the education market, Compaq saw Linux as ideal because of its free licensing and openness which are ideal conditions for students.

Compaq went the next step with us and entered into a partnership where we work with Compaq to make its own Unix software, known as Tru64 Unix, more compatible with Red Hat Linux. Compaq is also working on its own additions to Linux to make it more user friendly.

Marketing initiatives between the companies include Compaq's ActiveAnswers and Red Hat's Kick Start programs, which focus on training for the Compaq sales force and channel partners; documentation and tools to improve better service, performance, and ease of installation; and customer-focused activities such as seminars, trade shows, and telemarketing.

Enrico Pesatori, Compaq's senior vice president and general manager for the enterprise computing group, said the collaboration with Red Hat would enable Compaq to offer a mix of Tru64 and Linux technology for customers in a seamless way.

A key goal of the expanded partnership between Compaq and Red Hat was to ensure that programs could be created in a single source code implementation, compiled by either Linux or Tru64.

—◆—

On the "thin server" side of the equation, Compaq had launched a new product line known as TaskSmart, a collection of "server appliances" specialized for doing one task very well. The products were targeted at small business and ISPs. International Data Corporation, the market research think tank, said Compaq is the first big-name company to get its feet wet in the server appliance market.

Server appliances, also known as "thin servers," offer high performance, low maintenance, and ease of use and installation. Such products were bound to change the dynamics of the market, IDC analysts said.

While continuing to gain share in the server market, a market research study by Dataquest Inc. shows that Linux servers are expected to have an even larger impact on the worldwide server appliance market. By 2003, Dataquest forecasts that Linux servers will account for approximately 24 percent of worldwide server appliance revenue, or $3.8 billion. That's 14 percent of all server appliance machines sold, or 1.1 million units. By the same year, Linux on traditional servers will represent 3.4 percent of worldwide revenue, or $1.9 billion, Dataquest predicted. (That's 8.1 percent of traditional server shipments, or 450,000 units.)

"In the server appliance market, we believe Linux is becoming a credible and favorite operating system used by server appliance vendors," said Dataquest analyst Kimball Brown. "Not only is Linux free, but the support and continual upgrade of Linux off-loads the appliance maker from having to support its own operating system, further cutting costs."

Because the operating system is so low cost, he said, the vendor can either offer a lower price for the solution, which is good for reaching small business and workgroup markets, or realize increased margins.

At the same time, server appliance sales would likely take a chunk out of low-end server sales at Compaq and other companies, "cannibalizing" their server lines. Such cannibalization is always a risk when companies entering new markets with category-breaking computers. They stand to eat into part of their older markets while entering a new market that is potentially much higher growth.

Although Compaq is the first big-name player to offer server appliances, many smaller companies have been working at it for years, including Cobalt, Auspex, Network Appliance, and others.

Hewlett-Packard was also eyeing the server appliance market, and saw Linux as the good candidate for such machines because of its low cost and Internet abilities.

Server appliance manufacturers were already using Linux as the foundation for their products. In response, Microsoft was scrambling to get a new version of Windows NT on the market known as Windows Appliance Server.

Interestingly, Compaq's biggest competition was seen by analysts as being neither from the smaller server companies nor from traditional competitors such as HP, Dell, and IBM. This time, the competition was coming from a totally different rival—Intel Corp. Intel sells its own Intel-branded systems in Asia and sells kits to any "white box" manufacturer of generic computers. (This channel of Intel customers was the one that originally inspired Intel's investment in Linux.)

It is not surprising that both Intel and Compaq became investors in Red Hat.

———

Compaq and others initially began offering their existing computers with Linux, but were increasingly recognizing the operating system's potential on Internet appliances.

Compaq researchers have developed at its Palo Alto, California, labs a Linux-based handheld computer called the Itsy. To create the prototype, they modified the Linux operating system and put it on a computer that is slightly smaller than a PalmPilot. About 75 prototypes were created as an exploration in handheld and wearable computers. These prototypes would influence the development of future products. From the start, one of the obvious benefits in using Linux with this product was that it was royalty free; Compaq did not have to pay us or anyone else a fee for every Itsy that contained Linux. Computer makers also did not have to depend on an operating system vendor like Microsoft to give them access to a new operating system in order to introduce new types of computers.

The Itsy is an extremely simple device. It features a touch screen and a few buttons, and uses a 200-MHz StrongARM processor and has a 320×200 pixel screen. It also comes with a microphone, speaker, and infrared port.

The Itsy can run personal digital assistant software such as email, and also plays the popular video game Doom, with the player navigating through the video game universe by tilting the Itsy forward and back. Some Compaq insiders call this technology "rock 'n' scroll." The Itsy's graphical environment was powered by software from a startup called Transvirtual. Compaq, in keeping with the open source nature of Linux, also says its kernel for Itsy is available to anyone who wants it, seeing that any modifications made to Linux must always be released back to the open source community.

Computers like the Itsy and other "thin client" systems—computers tied to a central server—as well as television set-top boxes, are excellent candidates for Linux. Even America Online is working on a Linux-based system that will allow AOL users to connect easily to its network.

Compaq's goal with Itsy is to research certain issues about the development of such devices. This research will be critical to future products that will become commercially available. These issues include such things as power management, user interface issues, networking, and the development of applications for small Internet appliance devices.

The Itsy prototype actually offers considerably more computing power and memory than other personal digital assistants (PDAs) on the market, enabling demanding applications such as speech recognition. The fact that it is Linux-based means Compaq can quickly customize the machine for a variety of functions, identifying different product niches for a line of products. This project is just another example of the growing R&D investment being made by the major technology companies in open source software.

Open systems, and the open standards that concept is based on, are the most effective tool ever invented for the rapid evolution of technology, and the open source model that Linux represents is simply the most effective implementation of open systems yet devised.

I'm certain that some day Windows NT will be a good operating system. It is probably already a useful product for many applications for which one needs an operating system today. But, like Red Hat Linux, it is just so much technology. The world does not need more technology—it needs better solutions.

So when we get into debates about which operating system is more reliable, more secure, and of better value—which means lower cost of ownership—I could go into a long and detailed explanation of how and why Red Hat Linux wins handily in each of these categories.

But those arguments are as irrelevant as the argument on whether the Mac OS is easier to use than Windows. (Which, of course, it is.) As anyone who has spent more than a couple of years in this industry knows, the better technology seldom wins in the marketplace unless that technology represents greater benefits to the user than the alternatives.

What are the important benefits Linux users gain, that they cannot have when using proprietary binary-only operating systems? The answer, in a word, is *control.*

A great example of the benefit of having control over your operating system is that Linux is being used in millions of applications as an operating system that can solve problems proprietary operating systems cannot. One of the most important of these is connectivity. As AT&T found way back in the early '70s, getting proprietary operating systems to talk to each other is not easy. AT&T had at that time been trying to get minicomputers from a dozen vendors to work together.

AT&T reasoned that if it could develop a single operating system that could run on all the various machines it owned, connecting these would be a lot easier than trying to persuade a dozen different computer vendors to work with its competitors' protocols.

As you already know, this AT&T operating system project was called Unix. It is not coincidental that Linux has adopted all the Unix standards as its design blueprint. The same problems that faced AT&T in 1970 still exist, and in the same way that Unix helped AT&T solve its connectivity problems then, Linux is solving millions of similar connectivity problems today. For example, if you want to build a print server that would allow all your workstations to print to any printer anywhere on your network, you'd need an OS that could talk to Windows 3.1 machines, Windows 98 machines, NT machines, MacOS-based machines, Sun Solaris-based machines, Java-based machines, and machines running IBM MVS/AIX/OS2 and, well, the list goes on and on.

And as anyone who has had to manage a heterogeneous network knows, proprietary operating systems have a bad habit of not playing well with others. The reasons for this are varied, perhaps the most common being simply that vendors do not have much incentive to work on technology that aids their competitors.

Whatever the reasons, the operating system running this print server would have to be well behaved. Using Linux, the system administrator is no longer dependent on the desire, or lack thereof, on the part of the operating system vendor to allow him to connect with whichever protocol the machine he is trying to talk to is using.

Using tools such as SAMBA, Apache, NFS, FTP, LinuxConf, and dozens of others, a Linux-based machine can connect to almost every kind of computer system and network in use today and be able to perform the needed tasks without those compatibility issues. There are so many tools available that Linux is often called the platypus of operating systems.

But all this connectivity and reliability comes back to the primary benefit: with Linux, the users have control. Linux has taken the concept of open systems to its logical extreme. Where traditionally, industry standards bodies like the IEEE have worked on publishing paper standards that commercial vendors refer to and should follow when building their systems, the Linux development community builds real-world reference implementations that are capable of being used as is.

Linux is a real-world reference implementation because users receive complete source code under a license that enables the user to make changes without so much as having to ask our permission.

This is what we mean by taking the concept of open systems to its logical extreme.

Everyone using Red Hat Linux can assist in improving the operating system's ability to work with other operating systems, whether or not it is in Red Hat's commercial interest. It simply is not up to us and rightfully so. We essentially work for the Linux community and follow their lead. We cannot either intentionally or accidentally break our support of an industry protocol to make a competitor's product look inadequate. Our users would be able to see exactly what we had done and to fix it with or without our permission.

In previous competitive battles in the marketplace, due to broken standards and technology decisions made by marketing executives, consumers were often the losers. In the competition between Linux and NT, the consumer wins, because Linux works openly and effectively with any known protocol and standard, or it can be made to do so by the users themselves if necessary. The consumer can use both Linux and NT together—in full confidence that his or her applications will always continue to communicate, because, on the Linux side, users have the ability to modify the technology as required.

Again, I'm sure NT will one day be a great OS. But as long as it is a binary-only proprietary operating system, it will never be able to offer the benefits to its users that our rapidly growing user community has come to expect from Red Hat Linux—namely, that they have control over the operating system layer of the systems for which they are responsible.

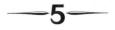

—5—

Heresies

*"Now I'm the president around here. So if I say a chicken can
pull a tractor trailer, your job is to hitch 'em up."*

—Jim Barksdale, CEO, Netscape

W HILE RED HAT WAS BUILDING ITS BUSINESS, Netscape was
being forced to change sneakers in the middle of a marathon, as
CEO Jim Barksdale liked to say. Netscape's investment in Red Hat was
the denouement in a steady series of market-moving decisions made
by the company over the preceding months, in an attempt to correct
its course.

In the fall of 1997, a fire was glowing in the living room of 54-year-
old Barksdale's elegantly furnished, Spanish-style adobe home in Palo
Alto. Joining the CEO for a critical strategy meeting were executive committee members including chief technology officer Eric Hahn; 26-year-
old co-founder and senior vice president Marc Andreessen; executive
vice president Mike Homer; chief financial officer Peter Currie; and chief
counsel Roberta Katz.

Barksdale, a native Missourian, and his wife Sally were known for
their Southern hospitality and the coziness of their Palo Alto home.
Nonetheless, these were uncomfortable times for company executives,

who were present to confront some of the most difficult issues facing the young company and its future.

At this strategy summit, the company began to weigh its options. In part, the changes in Netscape's business strategy could be traced in a series of missives that chief technology officer Eric Hahn had shot off to the Netscape executive committee between late 1997 and April 1998 that became known as the Heresy Documents, according to company insiders.

The Heresy Documents serve as a fascinating study of the shifting competitive landscape in the emerging Internet industry, and the impact of a monopolist leveraging its market power into the new market. They also illuminate the growth of the open source movement as a solution to the tyrannical environment many companies and customers were finding themselves in during the late 1990s.

As the group sat around the fire, Hahn gave a presentation based on one of his Heresy documents. Netscape was facing its darkest hour. The sales force had reported a severe shortfall in revenue for the quarter, and the company was anticipating its first round of layoffs, which would begin in January 1998. Netscape's business was being increasingly damaged by Microsoft's anti-competitive practices—notably giving away its browser, Internet Explorer (IE), for free, in addition to using restrictive contracts with computer makers and Internet service providers that effectively resulted in restraint of trade.

Netscape recognized that Microsoft had an unfair advantage: It had locked up all new PC shipments through contracts with computer makers that forced them to preload Microsoft's browser with the Windows operating system. Netscape was in the impossible position of having to break that stranglehold, and Hahn had some heretical suggestions on how the company might do that.

The last meeting held in the Barksdale's living room had been just as vivid. Almost a year earlier, according to those present, Netscape officers had convened at the same place to weigh an acquisition offer from an industry giant, the details of which, to this day, remain a company secret.

For sure, Andreessen and his colleagues had witnessed some eye-popping events in the course of the company's meteoric rise. It was hard to believe that only five years earlier Andreessen had begun his $6-an-hour software programming job at the National Center for Supercomputing Applications, while an undergraduate at the University of Illinois. Little did he know that the seeds were being planted for him and his future company to revolutionize the computer industry and electronic communications for businesses and consumers worldwide.

By November 1992, Andreessen had begun work on Mosaic, the first World Wide Web browser that helped make the Internet accessible to the public at large. By April 1993, Mosaic was released to the public, and in December Andreessen graduated from the university with a B.S. in computer science.

He then headed straight to Silicon Valley to work for the startup company Enterprise Integration Technologies. Months later, in April 1994, Andreessen left the job to form Netscape with co-founder Jim Clark. Netscape Navigator, the company's product for browsing in the Internet was released the same year.

Now it seemed like decades had passed, yet it had been only two years earlier, in August 1995, that Netscape had issued its initial public offering at $7 a share. By December of that year, the stock price would reach an all-time high of $75, and Andreessen's value would rise to $171 million.

But the beginning of the end came on December 7, 1995, when Microsoft announced its plans to focus on the Internet, frightening investors, who anticipated the market impact of the software giant and began to bail out of Netscape in droves.

Netscape's market share had steadily declined since that date. By the fall of 1997, Microsoft had launched its Internet Explorer 4.0 browser, and the damage to Netscape was escalating. Netscape would soon stun investors by reporting an $88 million quarterly loss.

Netscape chief counsel Roberta Katz would often attend Netscape executive committee meetings, and she and Barksdale had been shocked and alarmed by some of Microsoft's activities in the marketplace. Many of the other Netscape executives who had been in the computer industry for a while found nothing surprising about Microsoft's predatory conduct. They'd seen it all before; it was par for the course.

For one, Hahn had previously worked at Lotus Development Corp. He was familiar with Microsoft's business tactics, as he had seen Lotus Development Corp. struggle with Microsoft's leverage in the applications market. (In antitrust terms, monopoly leveraging is when a company uses its market dominance in one area to achieve dominance in a new market where it previously had little presence.)

"I've grown up with Microsoft, and this was just business as usual. I'd worked with Microsoft as either a competitor or ally on and off over the past 10 years. Newer folks to the industry recognized that this was illegal, immoral, and bad for the industry," Hahn said. Indeed, Hahn remembered the time Lotus chief Jim Manzi, in a speech at a high-profile industry conference, nonchalantly compared Microsoft to the Gambino crime family.

At Netscape, though, Hahn was probably one of the most pro-Microsoft people in that, unlike many Internet software engineers, he believed line for line that Microsoft software was better quality than that coming from other commercial companies.

Barksdale would sometimes agree, noting, "I think Microsoft is a great company, but they'd be greater if they did it all legally."

***

Now, the fire was crackling once again and Netscape was about to toss into the flames all its previous assumptions about its business model.

Hahn went forth with his presentation and suggested some startling tactics. Among them, he urged the Netscape executive committee to evaluate the possibility of taking 5 to 10 percent of Netscape's common stock and giving it to major computer makers such as Dell,

Compaq, Toshiba, and IBM, so they could prosper from Netscape's continued growth.

At the time, Netscape's stock was still very valuable and not yet in terrible trouble. Hahn suggested, in essence, that Netscape's only chance to compete against Microsoft, given its predatory practices, was for Netscape to buy its way into the distribution channel on new PCs. After all, Microsoft was not going to let anyone get a toehold. Netscape began to realize the lengths to which Microsoft was willing to go to win the browser war. For example, Hahn described how Netscape "would get weekly reports from a senior salesman in our company that somebody at Microsoft threatened one of our customers."

Netscape also considered offering a "Swiss" solution to computer makers who were terrified of disrupting their relationships with Microsoft. It was going to write a piece of software that PC manufacturers could substitute in place of either browser that would, in a non-biased way, present computer users with marketing materials on both Microsoft and Netscape products, combined with a download button for each browser preinstalled. In this way, after reading the materials, users could pick their preferred browser when they unpacked and booted up their new computer. Netscape, at the time, figured that most users would still pick the Netscape browser. Such an approach, Hahn believed, would have allowed PC manufacturers the ability to offer both browsers to customers in a non-biased way.

In the end, the solution that seemed most compelling was one that hit company insiders like a bolt of lightning, according to Hahn and others.

Before executives were aware that other factions within the company were thinking along the same lines, Eric Hahn made a presentation showing why Netscape should open up and release the source code to its browser, as well as set the price for the product to zero. (The browser had always been available for free as a downloadable product from the Internet, while simultaneously being sold through retail for a profit. Users paid for the convenience of not having to download this software. This download process, depending upon the power of one's computer system, was no small task.)

Being "open" was not a completely alien concept to the company, although many at first thought the idea strange. Hahn remembered when he first started at the company, in 1995 and early 1996, before open source was in everyone's awareness, Netscape took the position that it was providing the industry with "open software." At the time, of course, it didn't mean open source, but nonetheless it rang true with customers.

In other words, unlike Microsoft, Netscape didn't have any proprietary protocols or data formats: If you bought its server software and connected it to your client software, the following week you could remove Netscape from the equation and pick another company's software without harming your existing client software. Netscape did not lock in its customers. Barksdale had a favorite analogy: "The thing about open software is we're completely committed to it," he would say. "What your hear from other vendors is that they're 'supportive' of open software. There's a difference between being supportive and being committed."

Barksdale would explain, "It's like a bacon and egg breakfast: The hen is supportive but the pig is committed."

Hahn got a big kick out of that.

Barksdale's humor, now as always, provided some much-needed relief, as the tension-filled meeting proceeded. "It's not the size of the dog in the fight; it's the size of the fight in the dog," he would say.

Hahn recalled that the Netscape chairman never seemed to be at a loss for one of his outrageous quips, or some quaint Southern homily featuring any number of varieties of dogs and porches even during the most stressful of moments. Barksdale would tell his colleagues, "Your job is to run as fast as you can towards the cliff. My job is to move the cliff."

If the energy in a meeting was waning, Barksdale would pipe up, "If anyone has some data, let's hear it. If we're just going to use opinions, then we're going to use mine."

But Barksdale was not the only one who was sensing that the company's bacon was about to permanently disappear if it did not instantly adjust its commitments by introducing a new business model.

Hahn remembered his first encounters with Microsoft when he joined Netscape in November 1995, a few weeks before Microsoft formally announced that it was revamping its business to focus on the Internet. He had been with the company for two weeks when CFO Peter Currie came to him and said, "We want you to be the keynote presenter for Netscape at the Goldman Sachs investment conference. And guess who's going to be on stage with you?"

It turned out to be Jim Allchin from Microsoft, newly appointed by Bill Gates to head up Microsoft's attack on the Internet browser market.

The Goldman Sachs conference was scheduled for December 10, 1995. On December 9, Microsoft told the world of its new focus on the Internet. Hahn liked to refer to this as the "the day of infamy, when Microsoft turned the company around and focused completely on the Internet."

On stage, Hahn found that Microsoft was going after Netscape with a vengeance. Later, documents uncovered by the Justice Department would confirm his suspicions.

By early 1997, Microsoft's attack on Netscape had become the company's number one priority. On January 7, 1997, responding to urgings by Allchin that Microsoft integrate its browser into the Windows operating system because it could not beat Netscape's technology on its merits alone, Microsoft group vice president Paul Maritz responded:

"To combat [Netscape] we have to position our browser as 'going away' and do deeper integration on Windows. The stronger way to communicate this is to have a 'new release' of Windows and make a big deal out of it."

The new release, of course, was Windows 98. And Microsoft's contracts with computer makers stated that if they wanted Windows, they had no choice but to take Internet Explorer which had been built into the system.

Barksdale and Katz, newcomers to the industry, had never seen anything like it, and they recognized that Microsoft needed to be reigned in—what it was up to was not fair play. "Partly because they were industry outsiders, they were sincerely outraged by what Microsoft was doing to the industry and to our company in particular," Hahn said.

It became apparent that the only way to survive in such an environment—where the federal antitrust police inevitably did too little too late—was to change the game.

⸻⬦⬦⸻

Great minds think alike. While the Netscape executive leaders were talking about releasing the code, others within the company were thinking about the same idea. Independently, a number of managers inside of Netscape (for different reasons) had been entertaining the idea of open sourcing Netscape's browser. Within the company there were three schools of thought.

First, many engineers inside Netscape who had been with the company since the beginning had a "change the world" type of attitude about business—seeing that the explosion of the browser market catalyzed by Netscape, and in turn the proliferation of the Internet, had done just that. Netscape was hopeful that the moves it made next would have a beneficial impact on the technological and social landscape of the industry.

Engineers such as Jamie Zawinsky—a colorful character famous for his lopsided hairstyle featuring a shaved head on one side and a shoulder-length mane on the other—were passionately behind the open source notion. They saw open source as a way of quickly advancing the state of the browser.

Simultaneously, long-time Netscape employee Frank Hecker, a highly regarded sales engineer in the Washington, D.C. area, was in close touch with some of the company's largest government customers. He wrote a memo to the executive committee that, along with Hahn's suggestions, opened everyone's eyes. Hecker had been impressed with open source evangelist Eric Raymond's essay "The Cathedral and the Bazaar." In it, Raymond describes the cathedral as the traditional mode of software development, while the preferred mode takes place in the bazaar, an open place where anyone can contribute and which, he argues, is the more efficient way to build reliable software.

Hahn at the same time was also aggressively pushing Barksdale and Andreessen to seriously consider giving away the source code along with the free browser.

"A lot of people had come to this conclusion and luckily they were at different levels of the company. We had a sales guy with a lot of field credibility, and a bunch of engineers who obviously were the salt of the earth at Netscape, and we had my presence on the executive side, and we all had come to this conclusion," Hahn said.

Open source would represent a major paradigm shift. And many hoped in the long term it would redefine the entire industry.

Barksdale had at first thought the idea strange—it was completely alien to him, unlike others in the industry who were aware of the Linux phenomenon. Andreessen also was skeptical at first. But following those first meetings, momentum began to build. Mike Homer, who would become the general manager of Netscape's Netcenter, which would soon inspire a $10 billion takeover from AOL, clearly saw the public relations advantages of releasing the code, and the attention it would bring to the Netcenter Web site. He was easily convinced.

"Making the browser free and opening the source code was controversial because although the revenues were declining and we could tell Microsoft's behavior was going to cause them to decline more, they weren't at zero. And it was difficult to say goodbye to that revenue," Hahn said.

The open source licensing debate inside Netscape became hot during early 1999. The company wrestled with whether to use the GNU Public License, as created by Stallman's organization; the BSD license; a sort of public domain license; or perhaps the license used by Debian. There were four or five existing licenses to look at, or there was the "roll our own" approach.

Netscape's Hecker did a careful analysis of these various licensing options available in the open source world.

All of the standard license agreements published for use with open source software shared some common features, most notably making software "free" to users both in terms of being no-cost and in terms of minimizing restrictions on use and redistribution.

Hecker thought it best to use one of the existing open-source licenses, or modify one of them based on our particular business needs.

The choices included having no license at all, which meant releasing software into the public domain. Although the term "public-domain software" is often used loosely to generally refer to open source or free software, when strictly defined, public-domain software is software that has no copyright. That is, the copyright has expired, or the copyright holder has explicitly waived copyright. With no copyright, there is no "owner" of the software to grant licenses; hence, anyone may use the software, in any way, without any restrictions.

"Putting software into the public domain grants the maximum freedom possible to end users and developers. However, at the same time, it opens the possibility that one or more developers may take the software and use it as a base to create proprietary programs," Hecker said. If those programs become dominant in the market, then from a practical point of view, the software is no longer open source, even if one form of it remains available in the public domain. In fact, users may not even be aware that the proprietary products use public-domain code.

Because of this potential problem, most open source advocates recommend not making software public-domain; even developers who do not believe in the concept of "intellectual property" still advocate using the mechanism of copyright, if only to be able to use a formal open source license to ensure the source code to the software remains available. The GNU General Public License (GPL) is the best example of this (it will be covered shortly).

On the other hand, licenses like the BSD License place relatively few constraints on what a developer can do, including creating proprietary versions of open source products.

As Hecker explained, the BSD License was originally used for the Unix distributions released by the University of California at Berkeley. (BSD stands for Berkeley Software Distribution.) Since then, the BSD License or licenses adapted from it—the original MIT and X Consortium License—have been used for several other open source projects.

The BSD License officially grants the right to unlimited use of code in source or binary form, and requires that the developers' copyright notices and related material be retained. It also requires, Hecker pointed out, that developers be credited in advertising material, and includes legal language that limits the developers' liability.

Some licenses derived from the BSD License, like the original X Consortium License, omit the advertising requirement—which some have criticized. Others add a provision requiring that the software be provided "at cost."

Because the original BSD License was developed in order to release non-commercial software developed as a byproduct of university research, its legal provisions reflect this heritage. They affirm the academic tradition of giving proper credit to researchers—that is, the developers—and safeguard the basic legal interests of the university, or the organization employing the developers. Otherwise, its terms impose no real restrictions on use of the software.

From the point of view of a commercial software company, BSD-style licenses contain the minimum terms and conditions that an open-source license would need to have in order to be an effective license at all. From the point of view of open source developers, BSD-style licenses allow the maximum freedom in using the source to create derivative works. This includes the freedom to take open source software under a BSD-style license and use it to create a proprietary product for which source code is not made available.

As a result, many open source advocates recommend not using BSD-style licenses, preferring licenses that require that derivative works of open source software also be made available as open source.

On the other hand, as Hecker explained in detail, the GNU GPL and variants of it attempt to constrain developers from "hoarding" code, or making changes to open source products and then not contributing those changes back to the developer community.

The GPL in many ways occupies a place at the far end of the spectrum with BSD-style licenses in the middle and binary-only restrictive licenses at the other extreme, according to Hecker. Where BSD-style licenses permit essentially unlimited commercial use of open source software and essentially unrestricted creation of proprietary derivative works, the GPL is explicitly designed to prevent open-source software from being used to create proprietary derivative works.

It does this through "copyleft" provisions in the GPL that require that programs licensed under the GPL must be distributed without a license fee and with source code made available. It also requires that derivative works of a program licensed under the GPL must also be licensed under the GPL.

The GPL has a quite broad definition of what constitutes a derivative work of a GPL'ed program. It says, "any work that you distribute or publish, that in whole or in part contains or is de-rived from the Program or any part thereof," is a derivative work. Besides modified versions of GPL'ed programs, this clearly in-cludes programs that incorporate code fragments from a GPL'ed program or whose executables include statically linked GPL'ed libraries. It does not matter what license the source code of the new program was originally licensed under; the GPL explicitly states that when you distribute the same sections of code not under the GPL as part of a whole that is a work based on the program under the GPL, the distribution of the whole must be on the terms of the GPL license "whose permissions for other lic-ensees extend to the entire whole, and thus to each and every part, regardless of who wrote it."

Thus, if you use GPL'ed code in a proprietary program con-taining your own source code, you must make your source code available under the same terms as the original GPL'ed code. This property of GPL'ed code has led many to compare it to a virus subverting the proprietary "host" program to create more GPL'ed code, Hecker said.

The fact that GPL'ed code can "taint" initially non-GPL'ed pro-grams means that, in effect, you can use GPL'ed source code only to create other GPL'ed programs. This is a desirable feature if, like the Free Software Foundation, you wish to encourage the spread of the GNU philosophy, Hecker said. "It is also somewhat desirable or at least tolerable if you are creating an open-source product from scratch or if you wish to leverage others' GPL'ed code for your product, because the GPL is widely used and ac-cepted in the free software developer community and there is a large base of existing GPL'ed code," Hecker explained. However, it creates a problem for commercial software vendors who wish to license their technology in other ways.

Companies could also take an "artistic license" approach, by modifying the more controversial aspects of the GPL. Netscape would end up, in fact, creating The Mozilla Public License (MozPL) and its variant, the Netscape Public License or NPL, which would go further than the BSD and similar licenses in discouraging "software hoarding" but still allow developers to create proprietary add-ons if they wished.

"Since you can't use traditional software licenses and license fees with open-source software, you must find other ways of generating revenues and profits based on the value you are providing to customers," Hecker advised. "Doing this successfully requires selecting a suitable business model and executing it well."

There were several business models, a few also identified by OpenSource.org, that Hecker had identified for companies creating new open sources businesses.

"Support sellers" earn revenue by distributing media, branding, training, consulting, custom development, and post-sales support—instead of through traditional software licensing fees.

The "Widget frosting" model is for companies that are in business primarily to sell hardware, but that use the open-source model for enabling software such as driver and interface code.

The "Accessorizing" model was for companies that distribute books, computer hardware, and other physical items associated with and supportive of open source software.

"Service enablers" create open source software and distribute it primarily to support access to revenue-generating online services.

The "Brand licensing" model involves a company charging other companies for the right to use its brand names and trademarks in creating derivative products.

Using a "Sell it, free it" model, a company's software products start out their product life cycle as traditional commercial products and then are continually converted to open-source products when appropriate.

"Software franchising" involved a combination of several of the preceding models (in particular "brand licensing" and "support sellers"), in which a company authorizes others to use its brand names and trademarks in creating associated organizations doing custom software development in particular geographic areas or vertical markets. The company would supply franchises with training and related services in exchange for franchise fees of some sort.

There can also be hybrid models, Hecker said, in which the constraints surrounding open source are relaxed in one way or another. For example, a company might use both traditional licensing and open source-like licensing "side by side" for the same product, differentiating between different users—such as for-profit organizations versus not-for-profit organizations versus individuals—and/or between different types of use, such as intranet vs. extranet use, on one platform versus another.

Alternately, a company might license source widely to any and all users, and even allow "evaluation" licensing at no charge, but still charge "right-to-modify" license fees, restricting redistribution of modified versions in some way.

Although these business models are not true open source models based on a strict definition of the term, Hecker believed they might be workable models for some companies in some cases.

Hecker went on further, providing a primer for any company looking to implement an open source strategy. When converting from proprietary to open source, companies would be confronted with a number of issues.

One was code-sharing. This was when a company's open source product may share a common source code base with another one of its products that had a code base that remained proprietary. (This was true in the case of Netscape.)

In such a case, a company had to make sure that its open source development could proceed without complicating other internal development efforts. This could require special considerations in licensing, as well as a modular approach to enforce a clean separation between your open source code and proprietary source code.

Third-party technology may also become an issue when switching to an open source model. Any company's product may include technology licensed from third parties that appear in the existing source code base. This code would need to be treated specially in order to create a releasable open-source product. The typical options would be to remove the code entirely, to seek permission for inclusion of third-party code under a special arrangement, or to replace such code with open-source code providing equivalent or similar functionality, Hecker said. The presence of third-party technology also can influence a company's choice of an open source license.

Code sanitization will also need to be done, in order to ensure that source code is ready for public distribution. This means removing or revising any inappropriate language buried in the code, colorful comments made by programmers as they work, intended for internal viewing only.

Export control will also be an issue, according to Hecker. If a company is based in the United States, and products contain security and cryptographic code in order to obtain export approval, it will almost certainly have to modify the product for release as open source. All cryptographic code and security code that calls on that code will have to be removed.

Product development processes will be affected by a company's decision to release source code for a product. With these changes most of the benefits of an open source strategy will not be realized, according to Hecker. He advised that a dedicated team be formed which would be responsible for the open source effort. An infrastructure will be needed for contributions from external developers—including newsgroups, source code repositories with revision control, and bug reporting systems, for example. A company's own developers should be "customers" of that infrastructure, no different than any other developers.

There are some frequently raised objections to converting commercial software products to an open-source model enumerated by Hecker. For example, people will say, "If you make a product open source, does that mean you're no longer committed to it?" Companies can and should continue to have ultimate responsibility for an open source product. They can still exercise influence and oversight over the evolution of the product, and should continue to release an "official" binary version of the product, packaged for easy installation by end users and with full quality testing, product support, and branding, Hecker recommends.

Others will say, "But customers don't really want to have source code and can't take advantage of it anyway. Why would they prefer an open-source product over a pre-packaged binary product?" Actually, we've found that some customers do indeed want source code and find it of value. The other customers who prefer not to deal with source code can still use the pre-packaged "official" product binaries we continue to produce. Both sets of customers benefit from the improved product quality and enhancements resulting from open-source development, Hecker believes.

"Wouldn't this lead to fragmentation of the product into incompatible versions?" many in the industry ask. Indeed, it is one of the most common objections to the open source approach. "There is ample reason to believe that this will not be an issue, both because of the particular dynamics of open source development as they have evolved over time," Hecker said. "The open source developer community has unwritten but historically effective rules that assign control of an open source project, including the right to designate "official" versions, to a single entity—an individual, an informal group, or a formal organization." As the original developer of the product, a company can be the natural candidate to be that entity, assuming it does the necessary things to live up to its assigned role. (An example of this formal leader is Linus Torvalds, the leader of Linux development. More on him later.)

"What about the risk to the customer from 'rogue' versions?" Hecker said this has not proved to be a problem with open-source products, both because of public review and also because there is typically a single place—the original vendor—to get an "official" version that has undergone additional review and testing.

"What about providing technical support to customers with modified versions?" Companies can choose not to support modified versions of their product. That is, versions built from a different code base than your "official" releases. This support might be left to the general open-source community or to other companies providing such support as a business. Companies can also contract out to external developers to provide such support as part of their own support offerings.

"What about embarrassing things that people might discover in our source code?" Companies definitely want some "bad things" in their source code to be exposed, most notably bugs. Open-source development increases the chances that both major and minor bugs will be found and fixed.

"Wouldn't releasing your source code expose confidential plans and strategies to competitors?" Moving to an open source model implies to some degree sharing your product strategies with external developers and letting them influence those strategies, Hecker said. This implies sharing those strategies with competitors as well. However, at the same time this can result in greater public support for your strategies, since the outside world is helping you create those strategies.

Also, releasing source does not imply or require making all internal information publicly available; in particular, you can continue to keep a close hold on confidential details of your business plans.

"Wouldn't people just use our code and our expertise without our getting anything in return?" This objection is similar to the original objections to companies like Netscape allowing downloading of software over the Internet at a time when vendors saw software piracy as a major cause of lost revenue. But the benefits of a properly executed open-source strategy can well outweigh the costs, Hecker urged. Every bug discovered and fixed by a developer outside the company directly saves the company money otherwise required for quality assurance and software maintenance.

"What about competitors who might try to 'hijack' an open source product for their own purposes?" Open source licenses such as the GPL and MozPL can be used to enforce public disclosure and sharing of source code modifications. In the open source world, competitors must play by the same rules as everyone else, and those rules have evolved to minimize the chances of one individual or organization exercising undue advantage.

When examined closely, there is nothing strange or magical about open source development from a business point of view; it should neither be shunned as impractical nor embraced as a panacea, Hecker said. There is no one single model you must follow, and it is not an "all or nothing" proposition. Open source is simply a new way of developing, distributing, and licensing software. For companies that understand the economic, cultural, and political factors that go into implementing an effective open-source strategy, the open-source model promises to help businesses thrive in an increasingly demanding environment.

After Hecker's analysis, Netscape realized that the pivotal problem was the derivative work issue, which was the most controversial and difficult one to solve.

Many of Netscape's users were actually companies—customers that were selling products. Netscape was concerned that if it touched the source code in some way on its derivative works, then its derivative works also had to be openly released in source code. That would have been the case if the company had used Richard Stallman's purist approach, licensing the code under a GPL arrangement.

Netscape, while willing to drink the open source Kool Aid, realized there were other important issues in the commercial sector. Netscape had copies of its browser embedded in other products it was selling for its livelihood. For example, it shipped a copy with its management console that ran all of its servers. Did that mean that the management console too had to be released as open source?

Netscape wrestled with what would it mean for Microsoft, along with everyone else, to have access to its technology. The company had no problem with Microsoft seeing the software—after all, everybody was going to see it—and Netscape wasn't too worried about trade secrets or any intellectual property advantages it had. What company executives were terribly worried about was Microsoft potentially acting in bad faith. That is, "Netscape might put the source code out, and Microsoft might search for all the flaws in it and exploit them in almost a hacker way, to our detriment," Hahn said. "That was a big concern."

Moreover, there was the concern that Microsoft could do to Netscape what it did to Sun with Java. Microsoft could say that absolutely everything Netscape does to enhance or change its browser it will also put it in its own browser. The last point would be moot, however, depending on the license Netscape decided to use. The GPL license as extolled by Stallman, for example, protected against such things.

"Microsoft couldn't take some really cool thing we did with technology within our browser or with the rendering engine and put it in its browser because then its browser would have to be open source too," Hahn said. "And we didn't think Microsoft was going to follow us down this path anytime soon."

Many of these issues would not be resolved until months later.

———

On January 22, 1998, Netscape made the leap. It issued a press release stating that it was making its Netscape Communicator client software available for free licensing on the Internet. It planned to post the source code, beginning with the first Netscape Communicator 5.0 product release, by the end of the first quarter of 1998 when the final product was expected to ship. This would enable the company to "harness the creative power of thousands of programmers on the Internet by incorporating their best enhancements into future versions of Netscape's software," Netscape told the world.

At the same time, Netscape announced that its currently available products, Netscape Navigator and Communicator Standard Edition 4.0, would be made immediately free for all users.

The company said it would "handle free source distribution with a license that allows source code modification and redistribution and provides for free availability of source code versions, building on the heritage of the GNU Public License (GPL), familiar to developers on the Net."

Netscape would create a special Web site, known as Mozilla.org, where the source code could be downloaded and contributors to the code could post their enhancements, take part in newsgroup discussions, and obtain and share Communicator-related information with others in the Internet community. "Mozilla" was the open source creature born of Netscape's freeing its technology. Engineers inside the company saw it as "Mosaic" meets "Godzilla." The mascot for the project was a large green lizard that would soon be hoisted at industry conferences and executive speeches all over the world. Jamie Zawinsky would soon become a driving force behind the creation of the Mozilla organization.

In a conference call with reporters, Barksdale said, "Our business has evolved beyond the browser." Instead, Netscape would put more focus on building software for corporations and enhance its Web site as an Internet portal, a place where consumers can buy software and companies can advertise.

In the last quarter of 1996, about 45 percent—or $52 million—of Netscape's revenue came from sales of its stand-alone Web browser.

Since the previous spring, when Microsoft began giving its own browser away for free and bundling it with its dominant Windows operating system, Netscape's browser revenue slipped to about $17 million—or 14 percent of total sales—in the fourth quarter of 1997.

Wall Street analysts called the announcement a "brilliant move." At Merrill Lynch & Co, analyst Bruce Smith acknowledged that by giving away its source code, Netscape would enlist an army of unpaid developers to work on its side.

But accomplishing this would prove to be a bit more difficult than Netscape had imagined.

———◆———

Shortly after the announcement, Eric Raymond received an email message from a friend stating that it appeared Netscape had been influenced by his essay in its decision to open source its browser technology.

Raymond was surprised because he had never spoken with Netscape. In response, on January 27, 1998, he wrote the following email message to Jim Barksdale.

I was very gratified to hear last week that my paper, "The Cathedral And The Bazaar," helped Netscape decide to distribute Navigator in source and try to move to a bazaar development model. I think I may confidently speak for the entire free-software community in saying we are all delighted at this bold move, want to support Netscape in it, and wish you every success in pursuing the new strategy.

And yet, there's many a slip twixt cup and lip. Good intentions and promising theory need to be followed up by proper execution. Netscape's announcement has raised inevitable questions about how effective the follow-up will be. The same experience that allowed me to write that paper impels me to offer some suggestions, to which I hope you will give your most serious attention.

I see three major, immediate issues for Netscape's execution:
First: The exact terms of the Navigator source license are going to be a critical determining factor in whether your strategy works Second: Netscape now has a positive stake in the health and friendship of the freeware community, which it will need to think about protecting. Third: Having the intention to run a development project in bazaar mode is not the same as actually knowing how to do it.

Source license terms are going to be the first major issue. They're a potential minefield, because there is already vocal suspicion abroad that Netscape intends to pull the kind of flimflam Sun Microsystems did with the Java licenses—burying a whole lot of corporate control in the fine print of what appears at first glance to be a pretty liberal set of terms.

I guarantee you that if this even looks like its happening, it will backfire horribly on Netscape. The free-software/Unix community has a serious case of "fool me once, shame on you—fool me twice, shame on me" sensitivity about the Sun license. It won't be kind to anything that looks like another attempt to run the same covert-control game.

I recommend you study the Debian Free Software Guidelines at http://www.debian.org/social_contract.html. These were very carefully thought out after years of wrangling about the GNU license and its competition. They represent the culture's consensus on the minimum terms that can be called a "free software" license. Netscape's Navigator source license will have to conform to them to be credible—and you should not only conform but make a public point of doing so.

I am, as it happens, an expert on the terms and implications of the various commonly used freeware licenses (my detailed discussion is used as a reference at the largest Linux archive site: You can read it at http://sunsite.unc.edu/pub/Linux/LI-CENSES/theory.html). I would be glad to assist Netscape in developing its license.

The strategy you have elected makes Navigator's future literally dependent on the freeware community's health and goodwill. Maintaining both is now going to have to be a significant concern for Netscape. You aren't going to get your thousands of creative co-developers unless the free-software culture in general is thriving, and you won't keep them interested without keeping them friendly to Netscape as an organization.

Fortunately, Netscape starts with an excellent image to build on. So doing both should be neither particularly expensive nor difficult provided you get the Navigator source license right. You'll want to develop strategic alliances with leading organizations in the freeware community. This means, at least, becoming a corporate sponsor of both Linux International and the Free Software Foundation.

Again, this is something that you should both do and be seen doing. You want to do it because strengthening the free-software culture's institutions and cohesion will increase your advantage from the bazaar strategy. You want to be seen doing it because it's a clear message to the free-software community that you mean what you say about valuing what they offer.

Finally, there's a serious issue about whether Netscape will be able to run a bazaar-mode development properly. Without questioning either your intention to do so or the intelligence and drive of your people, there are still substantial obstacles in the way. I see two big ones.

First, running (or serving as the principal contact for) a bazaar-mode project demands a different and wider set of skills than running a traditional cathedral development. You'll need to choose your person carefully. The ideal person should have strong technical skills, excellent communication ability, and a well-established reputation in the free-software community. The person will also require sufficient political judgement to steer the project in such a way that cooperation wins for both Netscape and the free-software community. Finally, that person will require the trust of Netscape senior management so that he/she can make those win-win decisions and be seen to have them stick.

I cannot speak to the trust requirement, but filtering on the others I think I know of one excellent prospect and one good one working at Netscape right now.

Secondly, you may have a cultural-inertia problem. Netscape has better ties to the free-software culture than any other commercial outfit I can easily think of that is outside that culture proper. Nevertheless, it is all too easy for me to imagine an honest attempt to work the bazaar model being done in by internal friction and unconscious attachments to a closed, cathedral-model way of doing things.

I want very much for these bad outcomes not to happen, because if Netscape fails at what it's attempting, the consequences will be extremely negative for the free-software culture that has my loyalty. The free-software model could wind up so discredited in corporate America that hell would freeze over before it was seriously tried again. How Bill Gates would laugh! Brrrr...

Therefore, I would very much like to work with you and Netscape to make sure that your strategy is a success. At the very least, I can help with some consciousness-raising. I think Netscape's people ought to have a chance to see the Cathedral and Bazaar road show, backed with a clear internal corporate message that this is the direction you want.

There may be other ways that, without compromising my independence, I can work to strengthen ties between Netscape and the free-software culture to the benefit of both. I'd like to explore those possibilities with you.

Accordingly, I'd like to talk and meet with you and other relevant people at Netscape as soon as is mutually convenient.

Barksdale forwarded Raymond's email on to Eric Hahn.

Hahn contacted Raymond and asked for his help in crafting the open source license as well as giving guidance in other areas as Netscape made its maiden journey into the open source arena. Hahn perceived that Raymond initially viewed him skeptically, being a "suit" at the executive vice president level of the company. (In fact, Hahn and others at top levels of the corporation had literally never worn a suit during their tenures at the young company.) "He sent me this almost rude—'you couldn't possibly understand the issues'—kind of email," Hahn said.

Nevertheless, the two agreed on a date when Raymond would come to meet with Netscape's new Mozilla team as well as the other executives working on developing the new open source license.

Netscape's Jamie Zawinsky, who would be put in charge of the Mozilla project, had sent an email message to Raymond around the same time:

> Crazy times. I'm lobbying for a setup where there's a "linus-like" organization that stewards the public release in the usual free software way (despite being funded by / run by Netscape); and then there's a Netscape commercial client organization that takes code drops from that free organization, and productizes them (putting back the licensed and crypto code, adding other value, etc.) I want the free organization to be run by me and ebina, and not be dependent on Netscape's internal release schedules. We'll see how that plays out...

In early February, Raymond arrived at Netscape.

Bridging the corporate world to reach the leaders and the key contributors in the open source community was a challenge indeed.

"I mean, they're all great people, but the style here was pretty difficult," Hahn said. "Netscape being a commercial concern, and me being an executive VP sort, it was a little challenging to get the best thinkers all in a room to work on the licensing issues. But we did."

Indeed, the aesthetics of the two worlds were completely different. The schism existed not only between company executives and the outside world of open source contributors, but also within the company itself. But that was true for most Internet companies. The development organization is usually in sync with the spirit that originally gave rise to the creation of the Internet: almost a religious belief in the greater good of technical excellence. "Individual philosophical beliefs were held very passionately in the engineering organizations," Hahn said, "and 'management' is responsible for keeping the lights on." That was the culture at Yahoo and certainly was the culture of many parts of Netscape for a long time.

But Hahn and other executives recognized that what they were dealing with, reconciling the various management and engineering concerns within their own company, was tame compared with what was happening with people out on the Net.

At this point, Hahn told himself, "OK, we're really going to have to have a thick skin to make it through this."

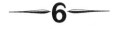

The Fish Bowl

"Linux is the industry's best hope against Windows NT."

—Eric Hahn

H AHN'S REFLECTION ABOUT THICK SKIN turned out to be accurate.

Following Netscape's dramatic announcement, a large number of business and legal issues had to be resolved. The largest single piece of work needed to accommodate a shift to the open source world was to create a license under which Netscape's technology could be given to the public.

Engineers also had some technical issues to wrangle with. The source code to Netscape's browser was never intended for release, so it needed to be reworked. For example, there were third-party products within the code that Netscape could not release. There were also government restrictions concerning cryptography. Cryptographic code could not be released freely due to export restrictions. In addition, the browser contained some proprietary Netscape technology that was too sensitive to be released. All of this had to be filtered out of the code.

Shortly after Raymond's visit to Netscape, Red Hat met with a group of Netscape executives on February 8, 1998 to provide some guidance on the company's creation of its new open source license. Richard Stallman and Linus Torvalds would also visit the company separately to provide their own views of the open source world.

This was my first visit to Netscape. The company had just moved into a flashy new campus consisting of several three-story glass and brick buildings in Mountain View, California. It was an odd place at that time; the new campus should have been cause for celebration, but instead, as a result of the unexpected losses for the last quarter and recent layoffs, the air on campus was dismal.

Erik Troan and I walked by rows of empty cubicles. These were supposed to have been filled with new hires; instead, they were vacant with no likelihood of being filled anytime soon.

Netscape was now devising the license it wanted to use, the NPL, or Netscape Public License, modeled in part after Stallman's groundbreaking GPL. Mozilla would be the core of the Netscape Navigator Web browser minus all the proprietary add-on tools Netscape had licensed from other vendors.

Netscape's licensing team, including Jamie Zawinsky; Mike Shaver, an engineer in his early 20s; corporate counsel; and several other staff, spent time with us discussing the issues.

The Netscape licensing committee had stated its desire to license its browser technology "in the spirit of the GPL." When we asked why not just use the GPL itself, they explained that there were a series of issues they were facing that were not possible in the GPL. For example, one issue was the right to integrate proprietary software into the browser. Netscape's products, like most large companies, licensed proprietary pieces of software from other companies to incorporate into its final product.

Netscape also wanted the right to be able to stop making future versions of the Netscape code available under the open source license, if it chose to do so. Netscape was not attempting to withdraw code it had already released, it just wanted the option, if the open source experiment failed, to go back to a closed-source strategy for its browsers. This appeared to be a condition its board of directors was requiring.

Another goal for its license was the ability to let third-party developers use Mozilla as the basis for their own browsing efforts. Microsoft's Internet Explorer had garnered a strong following among developers due to the modular structure of the browser, and Microsoft's encouragement of embedding that browser in other applications. Netscape wanted to counter that with Mozilla, and it needed a license that was compatible with that goal.

Erik Troan and I leaned on Netscape to adopt a license that was as close to the GPL as possible if it really wanted to create a cooperative development community around its browser. We believed that using a license that kept Netscape in control of the software would undermine the goal of encouraging non-Netscape engineers to help develop the code. Netscape executives understood the importance of this concept and became supportive of this view.

Netscape's decision to open source its code was a welcome surprise for us. Earlier, Erik Troan, Donnie Barnes, and other Red Hat engineers had been involved in online discussions with Netscape engineers Mike Shaver and Zawinsky on these and other topics concerning its browser strategies.

At one point we thought our business model might be damaged or ineffective if we couldn't convince other companies like Netscape to participate in the open source world.

Back in the summer of 1997, I spent a lot of time negotiating with Netscape to purchase a license that would allow Red Hat to ship a bundled version of the Netscape Navigator browser to our customers. (In the fall of 1996, we had licensed the Spyglass browser and had shipped it from then through the spring of 1997, but Spyglass was not keeping its browser technology current with industry standards, so we needed another option.)

Because Netscape engineers were Linux enthusiasts, they maintained a version of Navigator for Linux, but required Linux users to download the browser separately. Vendors of Linux CD-ROMs were not allowed to distribute the Netscape browsers without permission and payment to Netscape.

Negotiations with Netscape went on. Although impressed by the quantity of browser licenses we were willing to commit to shipping in a 12-month period—250,000 to 500,000 units—Netscape was not impressed by the price we were willing to pay. They initially wanted $20 a unit but we were only willing to pay $4 per unit.

Our flagship product at this time, Red Hat Linux 3.03, sold at full retail for $49.95, but through distribution we earned as little as $19.78 per unit. At the time, the vast majority of our customers were students and hobbyists who were extremely price sensitive. We considered raising the price in order to accommodate the additional $4 per unit—however, we did not think our core customers would be willing to accept much of a price increase for a product they could download at no cost off the Net.

By July, Netscape was willing to consider $8 per unit, and we continued negotiating over whether we could afford to pay more than $4 and whether Netscape could offer less than $8.

These negotiations came to a sudden stop, however, when Netscape called to tell me it had just signed an exclusive contract for its Linux browser technology on Linux with Caldera. Netscape suggested I purchase the browser licenses we were interested in from Caldera directly.

Unfortunately, Caldera told me it had agreed to pay Netscape $12 a copy, which meant the best it could offer Red Hat was in the $14 to $16 range. Needless to say, these prices were not acceptable and we were forced to consider alternatives.

The preferred solution was to have the open source community build a viable, competitive, open-source implementation of a browser, the same way the Apache team built a very competitive Web server. But Netscape's policy of building its browsers for Linux and making these available at no cost eliminated a lot of the incentive to build an open source browser.

By September 1997 we were beginning to doubt the future of open source software development, and in particular Red Hat's ability to build competitive Linux-based operating systems exclusively using open source software. If Web browsers, one of the most popular applications for Linux, were only available on a proprietary basis, how could we compete without including one?

We discussed this critical issue at the technical and marketing management level within Red Hat, as well as at a board meeting between myself, Marc Ewing, and Frank Batten Jr.

What surprised Ewing and me was Frank's unquestioning support of what we decided was our only, although rather radical, option: Red Hat had to build a software development team large enough and with enough funding to ensure these features could be built with open source tools. If we could not ship Netscape, we would build our own browser.

This decision led to the formation of Red Hat Advanced Development (RHAD) Labs in November of 1997. Ewing was freed from all other development responsibilities, leaving Troan, who had been the primary developer of Red Hat Linux for several releases, with full responsibility for the Red Hat Linux development team. Ewing then went about setting up a separate office, and recruiting a team of engineers to begin work on these projects.

This was considered a radical solution because development teams of the scale necessary to build a competitive browser, and full-featured desktop, were not cheap. This commitment the Red Hat board was prepared to make was huge by our standards, but it was tiny by the standards of companies like Netscape, Apple, and Microsoft, our competitors.

Fortunately, Netscape would not remain a competitor for long. Netscape's January 1998 announcement that it would "open source" its browser technology immediately eliminated a huge development task from RHAD Lab's agenda. This meant its task would now change focus and be directed instead to specifically create an easy-to-use desktop environment for Linux.

In the end, Netscape created new open-source licenses that were a compromise between existing licenses and commercial concerns. These new licenses would enable other companies to license the code without fear of undue restrictions on their commercial product development.

As scheduled, on March 31, 1998, the company posted the source code for its browser technology on the Internet, on the mozilla.org Web site. It did so by releasing the code under two different license types, the Netscape Public License (NPL) for developers wishing to make changes to the code, and the Mozilla Public License (MozPL) for anyone wishing simply to add new code. The code would be available in C and C++, the standard programming languages for most modern software.

The company made freely available more than 1.5 million lines of code, representing the basic recipe for its Navigator browser, which Netscape engineers had toiled over for more than three years.

In a move that surprised everyone, including Netscape engineers who had carefully removed cryptographic code from the software, less than a month after the source code was released, an Anglo-Australian group of software engineers known as the Mozilla Crypto Group, did what the U.S. government told Netscape it couldn't do. The group added full-strength encryption to an international version of Netscape's Web browser, and made available Linux and Windows versions of this browser.

They nicknamed it Cryptozilla. The Mozilla Crypto Group, made up of 12 programmers working over the Internet—nine in Australia and three in the UK—had a binary, encryption-free version of the code for Linux up and running in less than two hours after they downloaded it from the mozilla.org site. Versions for other operating systems—Windows 95 and NT, Sun's Solaris, and DEC's Unix, then followed.

Fifteen hours after the source code release, a fully crypto-enabled version of Mozilla for Linux was released by the group in source-code form. The following day, the group announced the availability of a Windows 95 and Windows NT binary version of Cryptozilla.

In the U.S., companies had been restricted from selling full-strength encryption technology outside the U.S. for national security reasons, though many in the industry oppose this policy.

The encryption technology used by the group was from SSLeay, the world's most popular freeware security library developed outside of the U.S. Therefore, Cryptozilla could be distributed worldwide.

The open source release of Netscape's browser technology had already had a powerful impact.

A few weeks later, on April 18, 1998, Hahn issued the final installment of his Heresy Documents. This one was known as the "Uber Heresy." It contained a proposal for Netscape's strategy for the year 2000. A full third of the document was devoted to Linux and open source.

In bold, on page 7 of the 13-page document, Hahn gave Netscape a litany of imperatives. He wrote, "Netscape should bet on Linux in a big way. Linux should be our reference platform for all server products. We should run NetCenter exclusively on Linux. We should give Linux to nearly all of our developers. We should support the Linux community publicly and privately. We should work to encourage all hardware and software partners to do the same."

Hahn's heresies were intended to be roadmaps and this one centered on the role of Linux and open source in general. It included an analysis of how the company would face competition from Microsoft; in fact, one section was titled, "Linux is the industry's best hope against Windows NT." This section discussed the five major advantages of Linux: It's free, it's technically superior, its source is open, it has more developers, and it offers better support.

Among other things, Hahn urged Netscape to get behind Perl, a language used by Web developers that can scan databases and documents and display the results in tabular form. (Perl is described by some in the open source community as the "duct tape of the Internet.") Netscape had been pushing its own scripting language, Java Script, for use on the server. His position was that Java Script "was a non starter on the server side and what we should have done is got behind Perl in a significant way," he said.

The Uber Heresy made some other bold suggestions, including that Netscape buy Red Hat.

It eventually led to the company's investment in Red Hat, which was announced to the world on September 9, 1998.

By October 1998, Barksdale and other executive committee members were embroiled in acquisition talks with America Online. Netscape was on a list of companies AOL had set its sights on.

The main asset that interested AOL was Netscape's Netcenter, the Internet portal. In August 1998, the companies entered into a deal that managed to bridge a rift that began when AOL chose Microsoft's IE over Netscape Navigator. The deal was a two-year agreement for Netscape to equip the Netcenter's Local Channel with AOL's local city guide, Digital City.

By fall, AOL approached Netscape with an acquisition offer. Once again, Barksdale, Currie, Homer, and Andreessen sat with suitors Steve Case, CEO of AOL; AOL president Robert Pittman; and Miles Gilburned, AOL senior VP of corporate development. On the Sunday before Thanksgiving the boards of both companies approved the $4.2 billion deal. By the time the deal was actually closed, it would be worth $10 billion.

The sale of Netscape to AOL was consummated in March 1999. The following month, almost a year after Netscape's landmark decision to open up its source code, one of the leaders of the effort resigned.

On April 1, 1999, Jamie Zawinsky called it quits and posted his resignation letter on the Internet. Zawinsky stated that although Netscape had managed to change the world by turning the Internet into a new communications medium, "Microsoft had succeeded in destroying that market. It was no longer possible for anyone to sell Web browsers for money. Our first product, our flagship product, was heading quickly toward irrelevance."

He lauded Netscape's decision, two weeks after its layoffs, to release the source code for its browser. "Here was Netscape doing something daring again: Here was the company making the kind of change in strategy that I never thought they'd be able to make again. An act of desperation? Perhaps, but still a very interesting and unexpected one."

Zawinsky was the one who had registered the mozilla.org domain name the night the decision was made, wrote the first version of the mozilla.org Web site, and explained to groups of Netscape employees how free software worked, and how the company had to change to make it work.

"...I saw mozilla.org as a chance to jettison an escape pod —to give the code we had all worked so hard on a chance to live on...," he wrote. ".....By putting control of the Web browser into the hands of anyone who cared to step up to the task, we would ensure that those people would keep it going, out of their own self-interest."

However, in the short term, that didn't happen. Netscape had not managed to get substantial input from outside the company, and the project was not making as much progress as it had hoped.

Zawinsky was bitter in his resignation letter. Some Netscape executives thought he was too harsh, whereas other engineers understood his frustration.

"The truth is that, by virtue of the fact that the contributors to the Mozilla project included about a hundred full-time Netscape developers, and about thirty part-time outsiders, the project still belonged wholly to Netscape because only those who write the code truly control the project," he wrote.

It took over a year for Netscape to ship Netscape Navigator version 5.0. Zawinsky had hoped that Netscape Navigator 5.0 would have shipped no later than six months after the source code was released.

Six months earlier, believing that the complexity of the code was posing a problem for developers, mozilla.org switched its old "layout engine" to a new layout engine known as Gecko. "By being a cleaner, newly designed code base, so the theory went, it was going to be easier for people to understand and contribute. And this did get us more contributors. But it also constituted an almost-total rewrite of the browser, throwing us back six to ten months. Now we had to rewrite the entire user interface from scratch before anyone could even browse the Web, or add a bookmark," Zawinsky explained.

On the positive side, he pointed out, "By doing development out in the open, and 'living in a fishbowl,' I believe that Netscape made better decisions about the directions of development than would have been made otherwise."

Netscape executives acknowledged this was true: In its first year the project had failed to attract enough outside talent to result in a production release of Communicator 5.0. However, it was still too early to judge the results of such a monumental revamping of the complex project. The Mozilla project now went far beyond Netscape as well as its new parent AOL.

Red Hat began receiving inquiries from analysts and others in the industry wondering whether Zawinsky's resignation, and the initial difficulties of Mozilla, would be harmful to the open source movement as a whole.

This was interpreted temporarily as a blow to the movement. However, I had a different take on it. It was a problem for Jamie Zawinsky and possibly for the challenge of "freeing" a large proprietary piece of code—as opposed to building code in the open source model in the first place.

Closed software-development teams take all sorts of shortcuts in their code that can result in very complex and difficult to read "spaghetti code." When you then give others access to this code, it's difficult for them to learn how things work, which in turn hampers their ability to contribute.

A project built in the open, on a cooperative basis, by a team of peers ensures that the code—although in no way perfect—is at least clear enough for others to follow the logic and make contributions.

Any failure of the Mozilla project stems from taking huge amounts of complex C++ code that was written behind closed doors and then "freeing" that code.

On the other hand, most successful open-source projects start out as open source projects. The benefit to this approach is that open-source engineers typically write very clean code because they cannot be bothered to document it. In effect, they simply let the other developers "read the code" instead of reading the documentation that explains the code.

In addition, open-source projects are, by necessity, very modular, like individual pieces of a large puzzle. Developers need the ability to hack on hunks of code for a week or two without worrying about "breaking" what others are working on. Netscape Communicator wasn't written that way, and Mozilla had to be reworked to be compatible with that development model.

With proprietary projects there is much less incentive to write clean code in the first place, and there's certainly no incentive to re-write code just to make it clearer—a phenomenon that happens regularly in open-source projects.

Netscape's problems at the time reinforced a lesson I learned in the computer rental business—namely, to carefully manage the finances of the business for which I was responsible. Some analysts and even some of our board members have occasionally expressed concerns that Red Hat was being run too conservatively, in financial terms, for an Internet software company.

Most companies in our position would be raising as much money as quickly as possible and then "burning" through it in a attempt to build market share quickly. Instead, we've grown Red Hat largely within our ability to grow our cash-flow. We had raised money in the past—first from Frank Batten Jr., second in the September 1998 round, and third in the round that was completed in March 1999. However, these funds were all for working capital purposes—in fact, most of those funds are still in the bank.

As Netscape's Barksdale is fond of saying, "If a company doesn't have profits over the long haul, then it's gonna be a short haul."

—7—

Gods And Apostles

"Excitement to some degree can be detrimental to an operating system."

—Linus Torvalds

A T ABOUT 2:00 P.M. ON JUNE 8, 1999, Linus Torvalds stepped out of the office building at 3940 Freedom Circle in Santa Clara, California, into the sunshine. He emerged from his office at Paul Allen's secretive Transmeta Corp. sporting his typical shorts, sandals, and a Linux Users Group T-shirt with its penguin mascot.

Torvalds was taking a break in the "big blue room," as kernel developers liked to describe the outdoor world. Their breed was more accustomed to endless days in tiny rooms bathed in the electronic dusk of computer screens.

Meandering across the street to a Mexican restaurant, Torvalds mused over the phenomenon of the Linux explosion. To his lunch companion, he described his position amid the pantheon of open source gods as the "fat and lazy bishop" to Richard Stallman's messiah.

Torvalds, typically self-effacing, was perplexed by the barrage of publicity and idolatry he seemed to be attracting of late. Things had come a long way since the time, eight years earlier, when he was a 21-year-old student at Helsinki University tinkering on a 386 personal computer with a version of Unix. He couldn't afford to buy a Unix operating system for his machine, so he created a new kernel to be used with pieces of Richard Stallman's free GNU Unix-like operating system. The new system was dubbed Linux.

Code contributors in the early days took Torvalds' suggestions with a healthy dose of skepticism, and continued to work collaboratively with him to improve the system. "When I started the Linux, people didn't take what I said for granted," Torvalds said. "They said: OK, he obviously doesn't know what he's talking about, let's do it this way instead." Torvalds is a reluctant guru, expressing misgivings about his fame. "People now believe I always know what I'm talking about," he said.

"I actually expect and hope that some of the personal excitement dies down because it's even being detrimental. When I make technical announcements sometimes people take it for granted instead of having some criticisms," said Torvalds, whose second language is English.

However, the excitement doesn't look like it's going die down anytime soon. Thousands flock to hear him speak at computer conferences and he is continually hounded by television and newspaper reporters from all over the world.

These were relatively calm days for the movement, despite occasional flare-ups amongst devotees who found it near impossible to be on the right side of the line that Stallman seemed to always be drawing in the sand.

Stallman, who was known to the hacker community as RMS—his email handle—believed that all software should be open and "free" as a matter of ethics. It was the right thing for society. Companies that kept some code secret and made some open were muddying the waters, Stallman felt. Others, including Torvalds and Eric Raymond and companies like Netscape, Caldera, and Red Hat, respected Stallman's position, but believed open-source development was right because it was a superior model for creating great products, not because of any moral reason. They thought it reasonable that companies might want to protect certain intellectual property rights while also participating in the open-source business.

Stallman was nevertheless a very important figure who has been promoting the idea of "free" (as in open) software for the past 20 years. He was the author of the major open source license, the GPL—also known as "copyleft"— which enabled some 120,000 people across the Internet to work together in what may turn out to be the largest public works project every devised. While Stallman's ideology and religious fervor about his views put some off, if one were to look back through history, that passion has always been characteristic of great leadership. Great leaders tended not to be middle-of-the-road kinds of guys.

In the open source community, "some people regarded themselves as evangelical crusaders against the forces of evil," says Eric Raymond. "Stallman was in that camp," Raymond adds, not without affection. Raymond, the aggressively vocal open-source evangelist, knew Stallman going back years, but did not agree with the "freedom" extolled by Stallman, though he was not against free software. Raymond simply believed that it was OK to make a profit selling software. To Stallman, this was sacrilege.

To some, RMS resembled a mad prophet wandering in the desert. Raymond considered the man a Jesus lookalike—as seen in Byzantine paintings—with his pale skin, thick beard, and huge, arresting green eyes.

Stallman even masqueraded as "Saint Ignucious," a pun on GNU. At one industry conference he was seen literally performing blessings over software packages in his St. Ignucious getup—a long flowing robe and a software CD floating over his head like a halo.

RMS had in fact met Raymond back in the 1970s at a science fiction convention before Raymond was a hacker, and even then there was rivalry between the two. "He was fascinated with my girlfriend," Raymond said. "He also became fascinated with the woman I'm now married to." Despite their differences, the apostles clearly had some overlapping passions.

Raymond had his own personal raptures about certain kinds of freedoms. He was fanatical about the right to bear arms. He was known to go off on tirades on the subject sometimes during interviews with reporters, and often took his friends and followers to a shooting range. Torvalds once accompanied him to his "Geeks with Guns" festivity at a shooting range during a Linux conference.

A curious photograph even exists of RMS shooting Eric Raymond's gun. Truly, freedom was in the eyes of the beholder, whether it be the rigors of open source as a business, or—in this case—the right to bear arms.

Open Source Initiative board member Russell Nelson felt in the end, the issue of freedom of software would be decided based on whether the open source method wins in the market.

"But you can't judge the issue of freedom on whether it wins in the market," Stallman argues. "Just like you can't judge the value of ethics based on whether we live in an ethical world."

"They don't consider it [freedom] an ethical issue," Stallman says. "Years of propaganda have made it seem natural for people to control the actions of others in a certain way." He is concerned that this not be the precedent as the masses increasingly become software literate and the explosion of the Internet continues. Freedom should be at its core, he argues.

"This is affecting everyone's freedom, and everyone using the Internet," Stallman insists. "Most Americans will be personally affected by these issues. The plan is to take away freedoms before people realize what they lost."

The term "hacker" has taken on a pejorative meaning because of the much-publicized activities of 14-year-olds trying to break into the computers of major corporate and government institutions. In the Linux community, it was a term of respect.

The earliest of this breed were MIT students in the late 1950s. They dubbed themselves hackers as they loved tinkering with the university's large computers. Stallman claims to be a direct descendent, having started at MIT's Artificial Intelligence Laboratory in 1971 at age 18, while a student at Harvard. The environment was one of cooperation and sharing.

Stallman had the aesthetics of a hippie. There was a period of time in fact in which he lived in his office, sleeping next to his beloved computers.

In 1981, things started to change. While Stallman was working at MIT, across town Bill Gates and Paul Allen were using Harvard computers to write an operating system for the now-ancient Altair 8800. (Linus Torvalds was a 10-year-old boy at the time, just learning how to program on such primitive computers.)

Programmers took Microsoft's first program, the BASIC computer language for the Altair, and circulated copies of it freely, as was the norm in the programming environment at the time. The practice of circulating software for free earlier had inspired Gates famous "Open Letter to Hobbyists," which ran in a number of computer journals and was first published in 1976. Gates wrote, "Most of you steal your software. One thing you do is prevent good software from being written. Who can afford to do professional work for nothing?"

The rest is history. Gates ended up selling a proprietary operating system to IBM, which became MS-DOS. MS-DOS became the standard on personal computers, with IBM's blessing, and Microsoft quickly locked computer makers into contracts that led to its eventual monopoly position. While the industry became increasingly based on proprietary code, Stallman continued to battle passionately for free software. He was the creator of emacs, for example, a free text editor, that is widely used and distributed via the Internet.

In 1984, Stallman began work on GNU, his free version of Unix. Much of the system became important to what would later become Linux. His work, including the creation of the GPL license, catalyzed the creation of software tools that in large part fueled the explosion of the Internet. Earlier freeware efforts also played a part.

In 1981, Eric Allman created Sendmail, an open source program that is responsible for routing 80 percent of the email that travels over the Internet. It is currently still maintained by thousands of online programmers via sendmail.org. In addition, Allman started Sendmail Inc. as a business in November 1998. For a profit, he sells easy-to-use versions of the open source software, along with support and service, to corporations.

Another important force in the open source world is Perl. It was created by 43-year-old Larry Wall, a former linguist who created Perl while at Burroughs Corp. on a government-funded project. The software is free, although Wall has sold 500,000 copies of his Perl manuals.

Another open source program, BIND, was originally developed at the University of California at Berkeley as freeware. It allows domain names like Linux.com to be entered as textual name addresses instead of machine numbers (called IP addresses, for example, 43.72.66.209), making it much easier for ordinary people to surf the Internet.

Apache, the group founded by 25-year-old Brian Behlendorf, got its start when Behlendorf was hired to build *Wired* magazine's Web site. In order to improve the Web server software, he programmed his own enhancements and circulated the results, with source code, on the Internet. Other contributors added their code, and Apache was created. The name came from the fact that the software was "a patchy" collection of code from numerous contributors. Currently, Apache is used by more than half of the Web sites on the Internet. It was chosen by IBM, over Netscape's and Microsoft's closed-source Web server software, to be the foundation of IBM's Web commerce software.

In May 1998, Torvalds took the stage at Linux Expo in Raleigh, North Carolina, close to Red Hat's office. He was giving the keynote address to a packed auditorium that normally held about 2,000 people. Red Hat's Paul McNamara had arrived to meet Torvalds for the first time. There was standing-room only and electricity was in the air.

An excited crowd edged toward the bare stage where spotlights shone on a podium. It was as if Mick Jagger were about to perform. When Torvalds entered the auditorium, a hush fell over the crowd.

He stood before the microphone and leaned over slightly. Suddenly the silence was broken. "My name is Linus Torvalds and I am your god," Torvalds joked. Pandemonium. The place went wild, with flashbulbs flashing and people cheering.

"I don't know if anyone else could have pulled off that line," McNamara said. "You get the sense he's a guy who has his ego very much in control."

In fact, Torvalds was mocking himself and the adulation of his admirers. While he exerted dictatorial control over what went in the Linux kernel, he did not view himself as being particularly important or wise.

Torvalds later had misgivings about his "I am your god" line, when he was criticized in email for being "arrogant." He was surprised people didn't recognize it as a joke from years earlier.

The world-domination theme began when Torvalds started giving talks about Linux in 1993 and 1994. One slide, which always drew laughs, illustrated Linux's growth over the past three years.

"I would say that in the year 2000, which back then was a long time in the future, we'd be the number one operating system," Torvalds said. "Everyone would just laugh and think the whole issue was hilarious. I actually have people who say that I shouldn't be that arrogant, that I'm the next Bill Gates. They don't see the fact that it's part of a huge joke. I stopped saying it because too many people started taking it seriously."

Unlike Gates and Microsoft, Torvalds does not receive a penny in royalties for his operating system.

Torvalds began programming at around age 10. It was the early 1980s and computer games for the most part did not exist. "The only thing you could do with a computer was write your own programs," Torvalds said.

He taught himself from books and manuals, and then attended Helsinki University, which he describes as "a traditional European theoretical university where my computer science degree is not an engineering degree."

Said Torvalds, "The main part of the teaching is not so much teaching people about how to create a program but teaching people about the idea—the most efficient way in theory to do certain things. You take that theory into account when you create a piece of engineering."

For a while, Torvalds lived the typical reclusive lifestyle of a computer geek, sitting in front of his computer for days and rarely emerging to socialize or even eat. Since the birth of his children and his relocation to the United States in 1997, his schedule and lifestyle have become more humanized, he says.

On a typical morning, Torvalds wakes at about 8:00 a.m. with his children, and sets about doing the only housework he's responsible for: preparing a cup of cappuccino for his sleeping wife, Tove, the six-time karate champion of Finland. "She doesn't get up before that happens," he says.

From there, Torvalds usually sits in front of his computer for an hour or two, pouring over the email that is clogging his inbox and waiting for rush-hour traffic to subside before heading to work at Transmeta. (It is ironic that the deity known for bringing openness to the software industry is employed by one of the most secretive companies in the Valley.)

On this day, Torvalds has a meeting at Transmeta at 10:00 a.m. and so must be sure to leave on time. Other days, his arrival is more free form.

Once he's at work, and after his meeting, Torvalds again sits in front of his computer reading his email from Linux contributors—some containing patches of code for him to consider—while also attending to Transmeta business.

Torvalds leaves for his modest home in Santa Clara at around 6:00 p.m., again avoiding rush hour, and spends the evening with his family. "When the kids go to sleep, I sit in front of the computer again," he says.

Rumors of Torvalds leaving the Valley to live with his journalist father in Russia are completely unfounded. His father, in fact, has been rather bored with his job given the Russian political malaise, and is thinking of returning to Finland.

Torvalds' mother is also a journalist and spends her time editing wire stories for a news service in Helsinki. These days, her son's name is turning up in a lot of the stories coming over the wire.

Torvalds' office at Transmeta Corp. is a 10' by 10' square with a window, two computers running Linux, and an avalanche of papers strewn across his desk. It is June 1999, and one of the machines is a top-secret prototype running a simulation of Intel's not-yet-released Merced chip.

Intel had earlier promised the Linux community that it would provide developers with early specifications for the chip, so that they would be ahead of the game in getting Linux running on all types of Merced-based devices.

The arrival of the 64-bit Merced processor would be a particular boon, since Linux already handled 64-bit processing on the Digital Equipment Corp. Alpha chip. (Today's mainstream computer CPUs, like the Pentium and the Mac's G3, are 32-bit processors, meaning that they can load and manipulate 32 bits of data at a time. A 64-bit processor like the Alpha or Merced, doubles the amount of data that may be processed in a single machine cycle. This greatly increases the output of the machine, in the same way that a pipe twice the diameter will allow twice the water to pass through it.)

According to Torvalds, Linux already has all the capabilities it needs to run on Merced. While other software has to be tuned for 64-bit computing, Linux's mostly server-based applications will run immediately. Linux was well suited to exploit the new chip's features such as MMX, fast system calls, and 36-bit physical addressing, which expands the potential space of installed physical memory from four billion to sixty-billion bytes.

"With Linux, whenever Intel releases a new feature, they can test it out in a limited environment before they make it publicly available,"

Torvalds said. "The fact that the Linux community does tend to be more excited about new technical developments than the Windows community means they have better leverage in getting their new features in Linux products."

At home, Torvalds has several computers, which also all run Linux. It has been some time since he's used anything else, and he is relatively unfamiliar with the workings of Windows. Microsoft has never contacted him, he says, although he has occasionally provided technical support for Linux to "Linux people who just happen to work for Microsoft. But that's not exactly common."

"Basically, I've been ignoring Microsoft and they've been ignoring me, to a large degree," Torvalds says.

While Microsoft may be ignoring Torvalds himself, the company is hardly ignoring Linux. Torvalds says the software giant is most interested in trying to "discredit" Linux, although those efforts have backfired several times.

Others giants in the Valley have regularly called on Torvalds to help solve their technology problems, as well as to provide guidance in new markets.

Intel and other companies, like Netscape and IBM, have sought Torvalds advice for their participation in the Linux marketplace. Long before its investments in Linux, however, Intel had asked for Torvalds help in fixing an embarrassing bug that plagued its Pentium processors.

First word of the bug came in the fall of 1997, when an anonymous message was posted on a Linux Internet newsgroup. It warned users of a bug in the Intel Pentium and Pentium MMX chips that would cause any computer to lock up regardless of the operating system. For some time, Linux was known for being the quickest to respond to required changes to microprocessor technology.

The bug took Intel by surprise. It occurred when a particular series of computer instructions, starting with the characters F0 0F, were entered into the computer. It could be used by saboteurs to bring down the backbone of major networks, and was a threat to Internet service providers, web hosts, government agencies, and university computer departments where entire networks could crash because of the bug. The Pentium chip would lock up and freeze the computer when it encountered this instruction.

Moreover, any user could potentially construct a program with the instruction and upload it to a network computer. When the application ran on the network it would crash the network server.

Intel wanted to make sure it had workarounds for the bug before alerting the public. Earlier, Intel had a division bug that plagued the Pentium and created a PR disaster. "Intel is very sensitive to the PR issues," Torvalds said, "and tried to work with a lot of different manufacturers on making sure all the vendors had workarounds for the bug. They wanted to be fairly quiet about the bug and the exact details until they had completely verified that the workarounds were effective."

Intel called Torvalds in. From the start, Intel wanted to help in any way it could, including providing whatever knowledge Torvalds needed in order to create a workaround to this bug.

In an odd twist of fate, the Linux guru had been contacted by an executive at Intel, Sunil Saxena, whose first name had a strange association with his own.

Sunil was Linus spelled backward. He was head of Intel's Microcomputer Software Labs, and became Torvalds' go-between for communication between Torvalds and more senior executives at the company.

The Linux community had a fix for the F0 0F bug within hours. Other operating systems took days or weeks to produce a patch.

"Now they have a person who contacts me whenever they have some issues, when new things come up," Torvalds said.

He had been in the information loop regarding Intel's secret Merced specifications. "I don't want to sign any nondisclosure agreements with anybody," he told Intel. "But they are keeping me in the loop and making hardware available," he said.

Torvalds was having a surprising impact on some of the chip giant's long-standing business practices. Over time, in meetings with Saxena and others at Intel, Torvalds was told of internal political problems coming up at Intel regarding its involvement with open source software. As is true for most large software companies, employees must agree that any code they write will be the property of the corporation and not disclosed to any outsiders.

If Intel truly wanted input from the Linux community on what it was developing, it would have to change some of its long-standing policies.

"I now actually have a few papers that say code written by certain Intel people is actually not exclusively owned by Intel, and I'm free to do whatever I want with the code," said Torvalds. "We have the legal issues clarified." Intel is now actually contributing code to Linux that it hopes will be made publicly available.

Still, the issue is not one that can be taken lightly. Large companies have so many intellectual property agreements with other companies that opening up their code makes them very nervous. "The lawyers are very nervous about everything they give away just in case it contains some code owned by someone else," said Torvalds.

He adds, "It's interesting to see how, especially for a lawyer, the situation itself is not nearly as scary as the fact that it's new. Once they get used to the situation, it's not that scary anymore. When they haven't ever dealt with it before, they're like 'Oh God, I don't know what rules really apply.' And they run around like headless chickens."

Among the thousands of contributors to the Linux kernel worldwide, there are just a handful that contribute the most important code for the kernel. This code is passed like manna placed on the altar of guru Torvalds, who filters the contributions and has the final word on what will be accepted into the system.

While the kernel, overseen by Torvalds, is only a small part of Linux, it is like the center of the universe around which a whole galaxy revolves.

While Torvalds shepherds the creation of the development kernel, Alan Cox, based in England, oversees the production kernel. Cox is a large British man with a long mane of chaotic brown hair and a prolific beard. He is one of the few that Torvalds trusts implicitly.

The top tier of kernel developers includes about eight individuals. In addition to Torvalds and Cox, there is David Miller, a lively fellow based in Santa Clara. Miller has hair to his waist and is often garbed in plaid pants, a plaid shirt, and a plaid hat.

Then there's Ingo Molnar in Hungary, Steven Tweedy, and Ted T'so on the East coast. Torvalds also had his eye on a newcomer, a man named Andrea Arkangeli. Although Torvalds has never met Arkangeli, he is impressed by the work he's doing and the code he's contributing. "I think he's from somewhere in Europe," Torvalds said, noting that, like other programmers, Arkangeli's location is irrelevant because all the work comes to him via the Internet.

Red Hat has a very close relationship with the kernel-development team and funds the salaries of five of the top developers. Yet no Red Hat executive has ever issued orders about what they are supposed to be working on. This guidance for the most part comes from Torvalds. Worldwide, there are perhaps 250 programmers on the kernel development team, the vast majority working on testing. Thousands more contribute bug fixes and other patches of code.

The amount of time Torvalds spends working on Linux depends on what is going on at his job at any given time. Usually, it's 50-50, he says, but there are weeks when he does one or the other almost exclusively. Two hours a day at least are devoted to Linux-related email. "Occasionally, if there aren't other pressing issues, for a week or two at a time I may not be doing much else than organizing through email and other times I do mainly Linux for most of the day," he says.

Wherever he's employed, Torvalds makes sure that he has a gentleman's agreement that allows him to spend a portion of his work hours on Linux. "I made sure that gentleman's agreement was actually written down somewhere, that I could do work on Linux during work time," Torvalds says of his current job at Transmeta. Of approximately 200 Linux-related emails a day, a portion are patches of code from kernel contributors.

"Some of the patches are easy because they're from people I trust and they're obvious issues that don't require much thought, so actually its fairly unusual to have even a single patch that really requires a lot of thought. Its easy to say yes or no on the spot," he says.

Indeed, Torvalds talks about the ongoing process of developing the Linux kernel as if it were an arcane, evanescent art that defies being captured in words or documentation. "It really works out, without really having needed any real organization, and all of this has happened quite naturally," he said.

At times, Torvalds sounds like a Zen master discussing how to reach Nirvana. "Nobody sat down and said: OK. this is how we should do this. There is a strong component of being an artist, but at the same time there is plain engineering. It's important that it makes sense, that it have a whole, and that it be beautiful in the artistic sense."

But the pragmatic always comes out on top. "At the same time, as with a bridge, it had better not fall down," he says. "It's a mixture of black art and pure engineering."

Nevertheless, behind the scenes, keeping Linux moving forward has not always been a serene affair. About a year earlier, in the spring of 1998, the guru was approaching melt down.

An apostle had turned apostate, and was threatening to split the kernel.

Code Of Honor

"Architecture is politics."

—Mitch Kapor, founder of Lotus Development Corp.

D AVID MILLER'S BROWN HAIR HUNG in a long stream behind him, touching the floor as he sat in Larry McVoy's living room overlooking San Francisco bay.

Beside him sat Linus Torvalds, quiet and pensive, wearing glasses and his typical T-shirt.

Richard Henderson also sat with them, on the carpeted floor, and was as subdued as he usually was, despite the critical nature of the meeting. McVoy—a former top scientist and software architect at Sun Microsystems and Silicon Graphics—was puttering about in his kitchen preparing his favorite quiche dinner for the group.

It was the spring of 1998, and Linux kernel developers were working at a frantic pace in anticipation of the 2.1 release of the software. Hundreds of patches of code were being presented to Torvalds. The only problem was that the guru could not consume what was being fed to him fast enough.

Moreover, in the previous weeks, Miller, a young hothead and vital contributor to the code, was threatening a digital mutiny.

At the same time, McVoy, who had been Miller's boss at SGI before they both became full-time open source developers, had noticed that Torvalds seemed worn out.

After two years in development, version 2.2 of the Linux operating system kernel would be faster and would offer expanded hardware support and other enhancements, and Torvalds and his colleagues were hoping to have it ready by July 1998. (It would slip to January 1999, while additional features such as CD-ROM drive, sound card, multiprocessor, and console support, were added, and numerous bugs fixed.)

Threatened by a rift in the kernel, McVoy urged that the group gather at his house to confront the issues. While McVoy and others in the community credited Torvalds' unifying vision with the fact that Linux had not become balkanized to date, things were threatening to unravel.

Torvalds was receiving hundreds of code patches coming in for Linux 2.1 and was "dropping them on the floor as he got overloaded," according to McVoy. Miller became angry that his work was being overlooked, and insisted that the process had to change. He was going to implement his enhancements on his own and "fork Linux" if the situation was not corrected. If this happened, everyone knew the future of Linux might go the way of earlier versions of Unix—fragmentation would make it eventually fail in the marketplace.

Torvalds, Miller, Henderson, and McVoy now sat together over dinner while McVoy proposed a new hierarchy for managing Linux code contributions, and suggested that a source management tool he was developing be used by Torvalds.

McVoy was convinced that a better source code management system would allow Torvalds to surround himself with a ring of lieutenants who would report to him through a hierarchical tree structure. His lieutenants would buffer him from the flood of details and code patches coming in from other contributors.

In the new scheme, and while waiting for McVoy to actually create the management software, David Miller would collect Linux contributions from the Sparc community, for example, those who were doing development for the Sun RISC processor. Miller would integrate code changes and fix bugs before sending code on to Torvalds. "The idea was to try and have these guys screening code before it hits Linus, so there's a filtering process," McVoy said. Prior to this, everything ended up in Torvalds' mailbox unfiltered.

On the Internet, McVoy was being quoted by programmers for his line "Linus doesn't scale." That is, like most humans and unlike a computer, Torvalds doesn't get faster when overwhelmed. "He's getting slower because of his popularity," McVoy said.

McVoy had written the source management system Sun ships today, called TeamWare, and decided to create a new source management system called Bitkeeper to help solve Torvalds' problems. While targeting for use in the ongoing development of Linux, he also realized he might be able to create a new line of business with the product that would encourage the health of the open source world while also attracting commercial enterprises to the open source model.

McVoy had been a Linux and open source visionary for quite some time.

Back in 1993, he wrote a paper which he presented to Sun Microsystems chairman and CEO Scott McNealy called The Sourceware Operating System Proposal. It was passed on to Novell chairman Ray Noorda, who would eventually form Caldera Systems, a company devoted to selling and supporting a version of Linux. Red Hat was also heavily influenced by McVoy's paper when we read it in 1995.

McVoy was convinced that Sun was all wrong in its operating system strategy. Sun was in the process of converting from Sun OS to Solaris. McVoy considered himself a "Sun OS bigot" and, as an engineer, hated Sun's new OS—Solaris—with a passion.

In his proposal, he made a business case for open source software. He wasn't arguing that it would make Unix better, but rather that it would solve all the fragmentation issues of Unix and give it a fighting chance against Windows NT. He was urging McNealy to give away Sun

OS as a way of unifying the Unix market. McVoy and everyone else in the market were foreseeing the inevitable success and dominance of Windows NT, if only because Microsoft could deliver a common, unified NT standard.

At this point in Sun's history, the company was worried about having to pay per-seat royalties because its operating system was derived from AT&T Unix. Every time it made a sale, Sun had to send AT&T a check.

McVoy started hacking around inside Sun OS and removed any code that was AT&T-specific, similar to how Netscape later removed any proprietary code from its browser software so that it could open it up to the industry.

"There wasn't actually that much in there, and I made the system boot and demonstrated that it would run almost anything any other operating system would run," McVoy said. The rest of the code was free, derived from open source BSD code and other freeware.

In the Unix world, numerous companies had added their own enhancements, which meant for any particular version, companies had to port code from one platform to the next. There were at least ten major implementations of Unix at the time, and all of the implementations competed for about three percent of the computer market.

Microsoft had one implementation each of DOS, Windows, and Windows NT. The Windows NT system ran on multiple platforms and compatibility was guaranteed by virtue of one source base, McVoy said.

In the Microsoft world, since there was only one supplier of the Windows operating system, if you could run on one Windows machine you could run on all of them. Customers did not have to deal with differences between different versions of the operating system. Standards efforts in the Unix community had failed.

Even if NT was not a great product, McVoy felt customers would switch to it in droves while the Unix suppliers were busy arguing with themselves. His research showed that Unix developers were spending about a billion a year on operating system development. Much of it was spent on doing the same thing over and over again. Unix had become too acrimonious. Rather than working together to create a larger marketplace, vendors became "religious" about their particular versions of Unix. Each thought its version was best when in fact the versions were 98 percent identical in terms of the programming interfaces that were actually used.

McVoy told McNealy, "This is great. As long as the Unix industry is arguing, Bill Gates is laughing his ass off, thinking that's cool, you guys just keep arguing." McVoy felt that having one source base, and giving it away for free, was the only hope.

He predicted that a well-engineered, free operating system would be quite successful. At the time, Linux had fewer users than it does today, but McVoy pointed out that astounding things had occurred in the Linux community in the previous two years. He used the Linux community as an example of why the open source model would re-energize Unix.

McVoy wrote that "software that is widely available and royalty free is more useful and valuable to the end user than proprietary software." This would become a mantra for Red Hat. The McVoy paper was a key influence in the creation of Red Hat's business plan back in 1993.

At the time, Cygnus Support was the first and only example of a successful, for-profit business based solely on open source software. It made money by selling support. Cygnus' revenue stream was doubling every year and was called one of the "coolest companies" by Fortune magazine. At the time, the company had about 50 employees and sold support development tools, primarily the compilers and debuggers for GNU.

Prophetic about the values that would fuel the Linux explosion, McVoy assessed back in his 1993 paper, "Almost every good feature in computer operating systems today, including most features in DOS, Windows, and Windows NT, came from the mind of one hacker or another. Typically, the work was not commissioned by a company. It was done as a research project and then productized. Without these people, we make no forward progress."

McVoy went on, "This sort of talent, energy, and enthusiasm cannot be bought. The hacker community, which includes universities, research laboratories, and many people at private corporations, is interested in the best, most widely used, free software they can get. Software source code is to a hacker as speech is to other people."

For McVoy, it was a disaster that many in the business community dismissed the hackers as "nuts." To dismiss hackers was to dismiss products that produce financial reward, he believed. It would be far more rewarding to find a way to allow the business world and the hacker world to coexist and benefit each another.

"If businesses want the best technology, then businesses should move towards sourceware," he wrote, defining sourceware as software that is either "copylefted" or freely redistributable. It was not zero-cost software, but it was accessible.

McVoy had been a leader in the creation of 100 megabit Ethernet, based on work he had done at Sun, where he had worked for seven years. His ideas were often so ahead of their time that his colleagues sometimes viewed him as a nut, albeit a brilliant one. Sun never adopted his plan.

When McVoy looks back now, he realizes if McNealy had released Sun OS as open source, the competitive environment would now be quite different. After realizing his proposal would not be adopted by Sun, McVoy sulked for about a year. Sun OS was headed for doom, like other versions of Unix, he felt.

After a year of licking his wounds, McVoy switched to Linux, and began working closely with Torvalds. He wrote software tools for him and others to use for performance analysis and diagnostics of the operating system.

Torvalds recognized the value of these tools before anyone else did, and helped define for McVoy what other areas of operating system performance should be measured. As a result, better software tools were created and the Linux kernel improved. "There's this saying in the performance world: if you don't measure it, it won't be fixed," McVoy said.

By 1995, it became clear to McVoy and others that Linux was going to be successful. He began devoting himself to contributing as much as he could. "I tend to worry about problems. Once they look like they're going to be solved, my interest frequently drops off." He had been fretting over the possibility that the industry would have no decent operating system strategy, and decided he had to help turn the situation around.

"This was largely because I knew Linus and thought that guy is such an amazingly reasonable guy, he's going to make this stuff work. It's not because he's the technically best guy, but he has this skill others don't have. He has the ability to get good work out of people who otherwise would be losers," McVoy said. "They're people I would just scream at, and *do* just scream at! There's no one in the world I've ever heard of that's anything like this guy. A hundred years from now, people will remember Linus."

People are always asking me about what will keep Linux from fragmenting just as Unix has in the past. Earlier this year, in response to these questions I sent a memo to Marc Ewing entitled "The Lazy Programmer" or "The Young/Ewing Theory."

The more I talked with the players out in Silicon Valley, the more I needed to be able to point people to a paper that provides a convincing framework for discussion concerning this issue.

This paper would help corporate managers who had to take Red Hat's ideas upstairs to senior executives, armed with plausible explanations about why using Linux, and developing for Linux, makes sense.

In addition, we needed to convince people to either release code under a truly freely distributable license or keep it proprietary. We were going to be in trouble if companies started claiming proprietary ownership of code in an environment that started out as open source.

The paper is reproduced in Appendix B.

Red Hat executives sometimes mused over the serendipity of the rise of the Linux kernel. If certain key events hadn't happened to fuel its proliferation, the operating system never would have gotten off the ground.

125

For one, the AT&T vs. University of California lawsuit made serious operating systems developers, including NASA with its Beowulf project, which began in 1993, shy away from using code that might become the property of AT&T.

In addition, the fact that Torvalds was based in Helsinki meant that he had to adopt an extremely open development model. There were no drinking buddies within driving distance to help him, so he had to learn to work with people he had never met, via the Internet. The existence of the Internet at the outset of his project also meant that he had to learn to do things from the start in an Internet-friendly way.

It turned out to be a strategic advantage that Torvalds' native tongue was not English. This meant he had no intentional, or unintentional, biases about his collaborators. Contributions came from all over the world and in many tongues.

Many believe that Linux will balkanize the same way Unix operating systems have. But the forces that drove the various versions of Unix apart are working to unify the various versions of Linux.

The primary difference between Unix and Linux is not the kernel or any other set of features. It is that Unix is just another proprietary binary-only operating system. The problem with a proprietary binary-only operating system is that suppliers have short-term marketing pressures to keep their innovations to themselves.

Over time, the "proprietary innovations" to each version of Unix cause the various versions of Unix to differ substantially from each other. This occurs when other vendors do not have access to the source code. The Unix vendors' licensing prohibits the use of that innovation even if everyone else involved in Unix wanted to implement the same innovation.

In Linux the pressures are the reverse. If one Linux supplier adopts an innovation that becomes popular in the market, the other Linux vendors will immediately adopt that innovation. This is because they have access to the source code and the license allows them to use it.

In 1997, a debate began over which graphic libraries should be used with Linux—older software known as the libc libraries, or the new glibc libraries. This rift was immediately seized upon by Linux skeptics predicting the downfall of the operating system.

Red Hat adopted the newer glibc libraries for technical reasons. Other popular Linux-based operating systems, however, stuck with the older libc libraries. The debate raged for six months.

By the end of 1998, however, all the popular Linux distributions switched or announced plans to switch to the newer, more stable, and secure glibc libraries.

The dynamics of open source development creates a unifying pressure for developers to conform to a common reference point, or an open standard. In the proprietary world—including the Unix market—intellectual property barriers inhibit this type of convergence.

The primary benefit of this new technology model can be seen in the birth of the PC. When IBM published the specifications to its PC in 1981, the world adopted the PC computing model with enthusiasm. However, this was not because IBM had designed a better mousetrap.

The original 8088-based PCs shipped with a mere 64k bytes of main memory. They had an upper memory limit of 640k. At that time, no one could imagine that a single user would need more that 640k on an individual machine. Tape cassette recorders were used for data backup.

What drove the PC revolution was that it provided its users with control over their computing platform. They could buy their first PC from IBM, their second from Compaq, and their third from HP. They could buy memory or hard drives from one of a hundred suppliers, and they could get an almost infinite range of peripheral equipment for almost any purpose or application.

Certainly, this new model introduced a huge number of inconsistencies, incompatibilities, and confusion, between technologies, products, and suppliers. But as everyone knows, consumers love choice. Consumers will put up with a measure of confusion and inconsistency in order to have choice and control.

It is noteworthy that the PC hardware business did not fragment. Specifications have generally remained open, and there is strong pressure to conform to standards to preserve interoperability. No one has a sufficiently better mousetrap with which to entice users and hold them hostage by going proprietary. Instead innovations are made freely available to the community at large.

———————

These days, Linus Torvalds tries to avoid being distracted by all the publicity and hype surrounding the Linux tidal wave, and sticks to the practical business of improving upon a great operating system.

"I'm personally very interested in the technical side, but my interest in the technical side is not necessarily to make the most exciting operating system out there but to make the best operating system out there," he says.

"And I actually think that operating systems should be invisible, people should take them for granted, they shouldn't get in your face," Torvalds said. Sounding again like a Zen master talking about states of being rather than technology, Torvalds adds, "Excitement to some degree can be detrimental to an operating system."

To him, excitement means strange and wonderful things, which can be an exercise in illusion and distraction. "In real life, what you really want for an operating system is that it's stable and reliable and it does what you ask it to do."

The Seeds Of
New Markets

*"There's a lot of potential in having a lot of appliances be
Internet aware. I've been talking to various companies about
this and it's something that is coming."*

—Linus Torvalds

L INUX WAS NOW OPENING EYES in all kinds of markets. In the
spring of 1999, software engineer Larry McVoy had been called in
by disk drive manufacturers who were excited over the potential to re-
vamp their businesses for the burgeoning Internet arena, while gaining
much healthier margins. At the heart of their secret strategy was Linux.

What McVoy was witnessing is what many others behind the scenes
were observing as well: Linux was being recognized as a force capable
of changing the dynamics of many aspects of the marketplace, and removing barriers to entry in emerging market segments.

Businesses were increasingly noticing that, instead of being forced
to accept the features that big vendors such as Microsoft chose to make
available, their information-systems departments could create software
that fit their needs exactly. Some systems administrators, afraid they'd
be scolded for using a free operating system, had implemented it

throughout enterprises but concealed it from management. They were taking old computers out of the closet and turning them into high-powered servers running Linux.

Others were openly committed. Digital Domain, the company of film director James Cameron, used it to produce digital special effects for Titanic. The U.S. Postal Service routes letters with RAF Mail character-recognition software, a commercial program that runs on Linux. Sega was using Linux to develop video games.

By the spring of 1999, Linux had an estimated 12 million users and the number was growing fast, particularly in corporations.

Likewise, disk drive makers were seeing whole new categories of Internet appliance products emerging because of Linux. They envisioned Linux as playing a key role in this area of Internet appliances, and had sought McVoy's wisdom on the subject, being a top Linux programmer and software tool designer himself.

The drive manufacturers were looking for ways to differentiate themselves, and were trying to essentially turn disk drives into networking computers. They envisioned customers would be able to buy a disk drive all by itself, for example, in a little beige box. Inside of having a SCSI cable coming out of the back, the drive would have an Ethernet cable coming out of it. At the heart of the device would be Linux.

Indeed, most of the drive manufacturers were looking at porting Linux to the disk drive, which would turn the drive into a networking computer.

There was some fascinating political history behind their strategies. Microsoft's licensing contracts with manufacturers stated that if they licensed Windows for any piece of equipment that contained an Intel x86-based processor, then they owed Microsoft a royalty for every one of those devices since they were able to run Windows. Every product with an x86 processor carried a Microsoft licensing fee, even if a vendor chose to run another operating system like Linux on that piece of equipment. (While the Justice Department had found this type of licensing to be illegal on Microsoft's part in the software giant's dealings with computer makers, disk drive manufacturers still felt Microsoft was enforcing these licenses in the disk drive market.)

For that reason, disk drive manufacturers made sure that these new networking drives did not use any Intel x86 chips. Instead, they would be based on ARM or Power PC processors. "Microsoft is a huge bully, and unless people can see that the bully is going to get his ass kicked, then no one is going to threaten the bully," McVoy explained, noting that some drive manufacturers were afraid to point out this apparent loophole in the disk drive market to the Justice department.

Ironically, the company most likely to lose business in this scenario was not Microsoft but Intel. "Because who's going to run Windows on a disk drive? That's a ludicrous concept," McVoy said. "But running a stripped-down version of Linux on a disk drive is a very reasonable concept."

This was one of the reasons that Intel purchased Strong ARM technology from Digital Equipment Corp., McVoy said. So that the chips could be used in devices using embedded operating systems like Linux. Intel knew there was a perceived problem with Microsoft, who was tracking royalties for all x86 processors shipped in every product known to man.

These type of devices were not that different from the Netwinder computer that Corel Corp. produced. (In February 1999, Corel sold that part of its business.) The Netwinder is a tiny and very quiet Strong ARM-based workstation priced at about $700. The Strong ARM was also the perfect processor for the networking devices the disk-drive makers wanted to build.

In fact, the disk drive companies were buying Netwinders to use as development environments. Those machines were very similar to what their new disk-drive products would be.

The recipe was simply to put an Ethernet tap on a disk drive running Linux, and drive manufacturers would almost effortlessly have an Internet appliance that a customer could buy for $400 versus $1,000 for a low-end computer.

The idea was not as far fetched as some might think. Disk drives already had a significant amount of memory for caching, and also already had two processors built into them—one that moved the disk head back and forth (a specialized analog feedback loop processor), and a more general purpose that does head scheduling, disk caching, and read-ahead, and write-behind functions for the drive. That processor has typically been a stripped-down 68000 from Motorola, not very powerful—but powerful enough.

With Intel getting into the market, the Strong ARM processors were substantially more powerful and cost about the same as the Motorola chip. Since the drives already had enough memory, manufacturers had only to rip out the old Motorola processor and drop in the Strong ARM processor, which could perform the same functions as the Motorola chip, but with one main difference.

It could also run Linux.

Interestingly, as the market for "Internet appliances" takes off, experts say Intel and Microsoft are likely to find themselves more often competing with each other.

Market research firm IDC predicts the market for such devices as televisions, phones, and hand-held computers linked to the Web will climb from just 3 million last year to more than 50 million by 2002.

A lot of people in the Linux community are doing a huge amount of work on new types of devices that run Linux and represent totally new markets. I suspect we are going to be hugely successful in this area as well.

Linus Torvalds had also been called in by some giant electronics companies and asked to provide advice on the creation of new types of Internet appliances that run Linux. Torvalds is very discreet, and doesn't talk too much, which is why people trust him. He is often invited into secret discussions with outside companies because of that trust.

Torvalds sees Linux's role as an operating system on Internet appliances—where the user need not care or even be aware what operating system is being used—as the perfect outcome for the technology.

"It does mean that all operating systems become fairly anonymous to some degree, and that's the type of setup people should aim for," Torvalds said. "My personal opinion is that Linux is extremely well suited to that kind of environment, but my goal really wasn't to take over the world one day! I'm excited about the notion of, for example, being able to email my VCR from work and say: 'Hey, I really want to tape that show but I forgot to tell you.'"

"There's a lot of potential in having a lot of these appliances be Internet aware," Torvalds said, noting that tests with Linux for this purpose have been ongoing. "I've been talking to various companies about this, and it's certainly something that is coming."

Red Hat is also talking to a lot of these electronics companies about similar opportunities. A large amount of work needs to be done, and I cannot discuss these deals until the companies themselves take their plans public.

But the logical element to this is, if you look at low-cost Internet devices like Apple's iMac computer and how it works, that there's nothing the iMac can do that can't also be done with Linux. Linux can do everything the iMac can do technology-wise but with the added benefit of a much lower price point. In addition, Linux can also be much more tightly configured to a manufacturer's specifications for a particular machine. That's because the iMac is still based on a proprietary binary-only operating system, and only Apple's engineers are permitted to modify it.

Windows also has inherently difficult design elements when you start trying to forecast how it will evolve into the future. Building a windowing environment on DOS was a bit of an engineering miracle in the first place, and in order to do it, all sorts of bizarre design approaches had to be taken. The Linux community is not taking those bizarre design approaches into the 21st century. It simply doesn't make any sense.

There are a wide variety of business opportunities for Red Hat in the Internet appliance market. At a conceptual level, it falls into two categories. One is the engineering work. If a manufacturer building

Internet appliances was to use Red Hat Linux, for the customer it would mean there is a migration path to future versions of Red Hat Linux for these appliances.

That means after the buyer invests in one of these appliances, when there's a new kind of Web browser or new functionality in the server that the user wants to access, he'd really rather not throw out the appliance. Red Hat would offer its users the option of upgrading the operating system on the appliance. The appliance maker can provide its customer with the assurance that there will be an upgrade path available.

The other ingredient is marketing clout. It's all about brand. For the purpose of marketing these appliances, one of the things that sold the iMac was that it was a Mac. Apple had maintained a reputation for being the leader in ease of use. If any company other than Apple had come out with an iMac-like computer, it would have had more trouble getting the message out to the marketplace of its being easy to use.

Manufacturers are attracted to offering Red Hat Linux-fueled Internet appliances, because they retain control over the OS technology in their products, whereas they would lose control if they used a binary-only operating system. The devices will be so reliable and easy to use, that customers will have no idea what operating system they are using.

Open source is very much in the tradition of our academic worlds. There always has been an open source tradition within academia and research organizations. What has not existed prior to the advent of the Internet, and companies like Red Hat and Cygnus, is the opportunity to take what every research and academic programmer understands to be a better way of developing technology, and deploying that in the commercial marketplace.

Open source is also fundamentally compatible with the way Western democracies work. Try to imagine running our legal system on a closed-source structure, where every lawyer had to reinvent all the arguments because he wasn't allowed to use the preexisting common law without paying royalties to other lawyers.

If a lawyer today comes up with a new argument that wins a case in front of the Supreme Court, he can't copyright or patent that argument. Other lawyers can use that argument without so much as asking permission.

Open source is not so much a moral value system as an efficiency value system. As in the legal industry, our society is more efficient as a result of this sharing of our common legal heritage compared to reinventing it constantly. For whatever reason, software has evolved in a proprietary model where we are not allowed to share, as Richard Stallman would say, so we have to start from scratch every time we write a piece of code.

Computer languages are called languages because that's exactly what they are. While we will allow authors to copyright a book so you can't reprint their work and deprive them of the income the book, authors can't patent the concepts within the book. Others can paraphrase and refer to the authors ideas freely, and are free to build on new concepts introduced.

That is not possible in the software world, however, because not only are there patents and copyrights, but the source code is kept secret.

———

In the next couple of years, there will be an explosion in new types of electronic devices connected to the Internet that are running on Linux. The operating system will spur growth in numerous new market segments.

Over time, as the open source markets grow, it will be fascinating to see how the law evolves. Some in the software industry believe that software patents do more damage than good. Others are either pro-patent or ambivalent.

We are leaning way over on the side of software patents being an evil, or at least very damaging, encroachment on the efficacy of the software programming industry. There needs to be a greater awareness that patents in software are not a good thing.

Stallman's GPL license, although a great thing, needs to evolve. And there needs to be a lot of evolution of the law in this industry in general, as there may be more and more code from commercial companies published under GPL- and NPL-compatible licenses.

Linus Torvalds also believes that the world would be a better place without software patents. At the same time, he is respectful of other points of view, and becomes irritable when greed overtakes some programmers who had participated in Linux.

"I think anyone who does anything artistic or writes any code should have the right to select whatever copyright is right for them," Torvalds said. "Something that makes me upset is when someone comes along and tells me I should have used another copyright for Linux." Linux, of course, has a copyleft under the GPL.

Added Torvalds, " I think, 'who are you to have even the gall to ask that of me?' My opinion is if you don't like the license, go away, you don't have to use Linux, right? You don't have to make the changes. If you make them you're kind of indebted to the other people who made the system so good in the first place."

Torvalds says that patenting ideas in the software environment versus processes in a manufacturing environment, is dangerous. "Patents have historically been used to protect engineering kind of ways of doing things, so you actually patent a specific process or piece, or the end result of that process. Patenting ideas is dangerous. And that's what you're doing in software," Torvalds says.

"Right now it seems very few cases ever go to court because nobody knows which way it will go. Large companies don't even want to run the risk of having software patents be judged to be less important than other patents. So what's been happening is, in the commercial world, you use these patents as 'I'll rub your back if you'll rub mine,' a kind of psychological deterrent," he said. "It's a call to war on a mental level. And I don't particularly like it," Torvalds says. "My approach has been to try to stay out of the whole mess as much as humanly possible and avoid the obvious cases, like some of the obvious patent issues in cryptography. That's an area where we say 'let's not go there.'"

In other cases, however, he says, "If it's a random small patch that we came up with on our own independently, it's not like everybody goes through all patent applications and tries to find them. OK, if it's something we came up with independently and it's obvious, then it's something we can protect ourselves against anyway."

So far, he says, Linux programmers aren't worried. "Corporations, however, are another matter. It does show up as a worry in corporations that, on the one hand, don't like the patent system themselves, but on the other hand are involved with it."

Torvalds says that it will take a major change in the philosophy of corporations if a gradual shift in control over software patents is to occur. All corporations and individuals stand to gain tremendous benefits in the long run, he believes, if software code becomes as free and accessible as the alphabet.

—10—

The Genie Of Gnome

"I'm afraid the Linux world is changing. It is used to be about having fun and doing cool things. It's a real business now."

—Bodo Bauer

G NU MIDNIGHT COMMANDER is not some stealth weapon used in Kosovo, but a part of Gnome, the desktop graphical interface for Linux being masterminded by Miguel de Icaza in Mexico City. The Linux community has hopes that Gnome will make the Linux operating system as attractive to unsophisticated computer users as Windows is.

Just before the first version of Gnome was released to the world, late on the evening of December 16, 1998, de Icaza had posted a message on the Internet to his fellow programmers.

"Hello guys," it said. "There are too many enhancements in this release to be listed. I can remember lots of the new VFS code hacked by Pavel and Norbert. The usual load of fixes from Norbert. On the Gnome front, Owen, Jonathan, Federico, and me have been furiously improving the code. The Gnome version is mostly finished, it has some rough edges, but they will get fixed very soon...."

De Icaza is a slight young man with a larger-than-life personality. He works in Mexico City at the Institute of Nuclear Sciences at the National Autonomous University of Mexico as a network administrator, and devotes most of his free time to Gnome. It is his hope that Gnome will make Linux usable by "nongeeks."

De Icaza joined the GNU project in 1991 at the age of 18, while he was an undergraduate at the university. He worked on the GNU file manager, inspired to give something back to the GNU community because he felt the software was so good.

When Linux came along, de Icaza adapted it and GNU for Sun Microsystems' Sparc workstations. Others in the community began sending Miguel bug fixes and enhanced code for the Sparc machines running Linux. De Icaza was roundly embraced by the Linux community, which recognized him as an astounding programmer. But that didn't seem to impress the U.S. government, which refused to give him a visa when Cobalt Networks in Mountain View, California, wanted to hire him.

De Icaza launched the Gnome project back in August 1997, and its followers faced several challenges. A Linux desktop project actually already existed. Known as the K Desktop Environment (KDE), the Germany-based project was the open source project. The KDE desktop was tainted because it included proprietary code from the Q+ libraries that was not completely open. This was one of the reasons de Icaza was able to build such interest in Gnome and the GTK graphical programming libraries it relied on (recently the Q+ libraries have become more open).

Within a year of its launch, 150 programmers were working on Gnome, including 20 full-time workers. Red Hat also had hired seven full-time programmers dedicated to Gnome and the KDE desktop interfaces.

Todd Graham Lewis, who runs the FAQ file for Gnome, said Gnome is greatly improving the functionality of Linux, and is being enhanced quickly for this reason. Version 1.0 was made available for free at www.gnome.org at the beginning of 1999.

At the most basic level, just having our source code out there—and the arrival of Gnome—is an encouragement to application software developers. But it will still take some time for Linux to compete on desktop computers. A wide variety of applications for Linux for the average user also had to come to market before it would become attractive to the masses.

Indeed, the widespread availability of application software seems to be the only thing holding Linux back from becoming as popular on the desktop as it has been on server computers.

In the spring of 1999, Bodo Bauer, a 33-year-old German citizen with bright orange hair is sitting in a Raleigh, North Carolina hotel restaurant with Miguel de Icaza, and a group of other Linux hackers.

It is the occasion of Linux Expo. Bauer recently founded Zenguin, a tiny company devoted to catalyzing the growth of the Linux application market. Zenguin's first project: developing a "universal application installer" for Linux products, another great example of the myriad number of new open source projects getting under way.

The problem, says Bauer, is that "Linux is a moving target for application developers, with the various distributions."

Zenguin plans to introduce "a new layer"—a reference layer—in its installer product, so that any software package written for Linux will work on any version of Linux. A great idea, but with an amazing number of obstacles to overcome prior to commercial success.

Bauer had been using Unix as a computer science student back in 1992 at the University of Erlangen, a German town of about 100,000 where about 40,000 of its citizens were students at the university. For a short time, Bauer and his colleagues began using what was known as SLS, or Soft Landing System, a version of Linux circulated by Peter McDonald. McDonald, however, quickly ended up alienating himself from the Linux community for having "branched the code." That is, he made changes to the source code on his own, without sharing them with the rest of the community. In two to three months time, the once popular SLS was dead—an example of the self-correcting nature of Linux development worldwide. Bauer and his colleagues then began to use a version of Slackware.

Bauer and his four other colleagues at the newly formed company have been at it for a while, working with Linux almost since it was born from Linus Torvalds' 386-based PC.

Three of the five Zenguin founders are former workers from Neuerenberg-based SuSE, the Linux company that is to the German-speaking markets what Red Hat is to the English-speaking market. When Bauer worked for the company, he was one of the first employees when there was a total of 6 at the company. (The term SuSE is short for a German phrase that stands for Software and System Development. It's now going gangbusters.)

Bauer sees Zenguin's pending products as a "balance between the commercial and freeware" worlds.

The Zenguin Installer will be released in its initial version early in the year 2000, he says, and will be based on GTK, the same graphic libraries used by his pal Miguel, heading up the Gnome project.

Zenguin is in the process of lining up investors, Bauer said, simultaneously thrilled and nervous about the unexpected worldwide success of Linux. "I'm afraid the Linux movement is changing," he said. "It used to be about having fun and doing cool things. It's a real business now."

Zenguin is also a publisher of applications software, both open source and commercial.

To give you an idea of how application development for an operating system works, normally if a big software company wants to port over to an operating system, it'll go ahead and have some discussions with the operating system company about entering into a very large agreement to get support from that company so it can do that port. On the other hand, when Informix, for example, decided to port its applications software to Linux, it simply went to Best Buy and bought Red Hat's $50 box and got everything it needed to do the port. So it's an entirely different model.

Red Hat also has an Independent Software Vendor program where we give developers reference materials and other resources that allow them to be successful at creating Linux software. We also provide some co-marketing opportunities that help them sell the resulting product.

There are also efforts underway to allow Windows applications to run under Linux, through emulation. A product called VMware, for example, provides this function. The software is not as fast as native mode and one must create layers of licensing by running MS Windows on top of VMware.

Some projects may have an impact on proprietary vendors such as Microsoft. The Wine project is an effort to enable Linux to run 16- and 32-bit Windows applications without needing to run the Windows OS itself. Insiders say it will be a couple of years before this is finished. But when it's ready, Microsoft may be competing with a Windows clone that's distributed for free.

"It's very interesting in a lot of ways, as a technical challenge, which is the part that really fascinates me," Torvalds says of the Wine effort. "I've never had the time to get involved and I don't have enough Windows knowledge to be all that helpful anyway, but I think the project is interesting technically and from the political perspective too."

"At the same time, I'm not that excited about basing the Linux application base on emulation," he said. "That's what OS/2 did and as a result nobody used OS/2 because, hey, if you're running Windows applications, why wouldn't you be running Windows in the first place?"

At the same time, Torvalds believes Linux will avoid the trap that OS/2 fell into. "We are so obviously different...we have other advantages. OS/2 really never had other advantages, it was a slightly better version of Windows—but in the end they were the same, to all practical purposes."

Torvalds said he is supportive of the application development community for Linux by accommodating changes at the kernel level that might help applications. "Whenever someone comes with a suggestion of something Linux could do better, if it can be shown to be a major help for applications, especially desktop applications that Linux is lacking, I'm very receptive to those kind of changes."

Torvalds has outlined his immediate plans for Linux, including more frequent upgrade releases of the kernel. The previous release took too long, he says. Version 2.2 was released in March 1999 and version 2.4 is expected in the fall. Torvalds hopes to make each release more modular, with fewer changes in each upgrade. He says more emphasis will be put on smaller devices, which are increasingly being connected to networks.

All types of Linux companies continue to spring up, and many are addressing the rapidly growing corporate market for Linux. That market is the focus for a company called LinuxCare. Since March, the 45-employee firm has been offering around-the-clock telephone support for most versions of Linux.

By the summer of 1999, more than 20 small companies were selling computers preloaded with Linux—in addition to the giants like Dell, IBM, and Compaq. Among them, VA Linux Systems, founded six years ago, sells Linux-based workstations along with support and consulting services. It expects to double revenues every quarter for the next two years. (Open source evangelist Eric Raymond is on the board of VA Linux Systems.)

August Capital has a stake in Cygnus Solutions, the oldest open-source company and a supplier of development tools. Andy Rappaport of August Capital says that open source could create what he calls an economic discontinuity where, instead of paying for proprietary software, users will spend their money on services or add-ons to free programs.

Other open source companies have also attracted venture capital, though not as much as Linux companies. A group of private investors called the Band of Angels is backing Sendmail, which makes the leading email routing program. Although Sendmail is selling a commercial version of the software with a special graphical interface, it is also supporting the development of the free version of the program that is an important piece of Red Hat Linux OS.

———

With all this activity, it's no wonder that Microsoft is monitoring the Linux market with intensity. By the spring of 1999, the software giant had established a unit inside the company whose sole purpose was to attack Linux.

In charge of the effort was Jim Ewel, a director of marketing inside of Microsoft's Windows 2000 group. Ewel, like other Microsoft executives, is an expert at ferreting out market intelligence, and getting inside the strategies of his competitors. Microsoft was acknowledging Linux as a real threat to its Windows NT.

Linus Torvalds is not concerned. According to him, open source developers have one advantage. While the Justice Department showed during its trial that Microsoft had hurt its rivals by starving them out of revenue, or "cutting off their air supply" as one internal memo stated, the company cannot kill Linux in that matter. "We don't have any revenue," says Torvalds with a smile.

Microsoft nonetheless was ramping up an aggressive campaign to discredit Linux in the eyes of corporate buyers. In early 1999, at the highest levels of the company, corporate officer Jim Allchin, Microsoft senior VP in charge of operating systems, ordered his engineers to run continual benchmark tests on the operating system in comparison to his company's forthcoming release of Windows.

Some of Microsoft's surreptitious efforts have been an embarrassment to the company when they became exposed. For example, in response to a publicized speed test that showed Linux was more than 50 percent faster than NT on a standard desktop computer, Microsoft paid a testing company, Mindcraft, to do another test on a server machine. The Microsoft-sponsored test showed that Windows NT was 3.7 times faster than Linux on a server with four microprocessors. It appeared that Microsoft had rigged the test.

It was in April 1999, just after Red Hat had completed its C round of financing, that Mindcraft Inc. released its study, without disclosing that Microsoft had, in fact, paid for the report.

The headline read, "Microsoft Windows NT Server 4.0 is 2.5 times faster than Linux as a File Server and 3.7 times faster as a Web Server."

A storm broke out over the Internet when open source developers discovered that Microsoft was behind the supposedly unbiased report, and in fact had rigged it in a way that favored Windows NT.

Mindcraft had conducted similar surveys for Microsoft in the past, comparing NT with Solaris and NetWare. The results always came out in favor of NT. The NetWare survey particularly enraged Novell Inc., which accused Mindcraft of unfair practices and published a detailed rebuttal of the study and its findings.

At the hacker site Slashdot.org and Usenet news groups, the report was torn to pieces. It was determined that Mindcraft had misconfigured the Linux server used in the benchmark. The company used version 2.2.2 of the Linux kernel, even though 2.2.3 was available and had fixed the earlier version's problems (with TCP, for example). In addition, Mindcraft used a controller that is not well supported under Linux; another controller would have yielded better results.

The most appalling thing is that Mindcraft had spent much time and effort to specifically optimize NT to make it look better against Linux. NT was given a 1012MB swap file; Linux got nothing. The test was clearly rigged. (This was not lost on the Justice Department, which had seen Microsoft attempt similar "test rigging" right before Judge Jackson in federal court.)

Adding insult to injury, Mindcraft then had the audacity to state in it report, "We posted notices on various Linux and Apache news groups and received no relevant responses." The study added, "The documentation on how to configure the latest Linux kernel for the best performance is very difficult to find."

The open source software community, priding itself on providing information and help, was particularly inflamed by this twisted account.

Mindcraft also had called Red Hat once, with the unusual request for sophisticated performance tuning from a novice-level installation help line. It also had sent Usenet postings to inappropriate news groups.

Eric Raymond called Mindcraft's feigned attempts to get help tuning the system "at best, incompetent—at worst, cynical, gestures."

Linus Torvalds however, notes that, while he was at first upset by the Mindcraft debacle, he soon realized that Microsoft was doing the Linux community a favor.

The Mindcraft tests were "a temporary embarrassment to us, but I'm not feeling that bad about it," Torvalds said. "I felt bad at first. But when I actually started thinking about it I thought, what the hell, as long as I feel confident in the basics of Linux, I don't ever really worry that they'd ever find something seriously wrong that we couldn't fix. They're actually doing our work for us."

Mindcraft decided to do a second test, which again inspired doubt about whether the Linux systems were adequately tuned. So the company proposed a third, public test.

Meanwhile, Microsoft's motives were transparent for all the world to see. It was running scared. After all, in 1998, the Linux market grew from 7 percent to 17 percent of all operating system shipments, while the Windows NT market remained the same at 36 percent.

Subsequently, there was a bumper sticker going around in the Linux community that says: "Mindcraft: the best benchmarking money can buy."

―――――◆――――――

Following the Mindcraft debacle, Microsoft's Ewel and Linus Torvalds engaged in flaming each other via email. Torvalds wrote, "Shame on you," complaining that Ewel had rigged the test.

Nevertheless, Torvalds insists that Microsoft's intense scrutiny will result in flaws beginning to be discovered in Linux, which is not a bad thing. "If they look for them, they will find them," he said. "And if you search for things that you do well, you will find them."

Torvalds laughs with satisfaction. "They're finding out weaknesses for us so that we can fix them. And that's kind of ironic in itself. Don't tell them!" he says.

But such attack campaigns on the part of Microsoft did not surprise Red Hat. After all, Microsoft had engaged in other efforts to try and dampen Red Hat's success.

While in the past Microsoft has used blatant strong-arm tactics (and sometimes outright bribery, as the DOJ has tried to show) to force companies to refrain from using competing technology, Microsoft is clearly feeling some constraints given the Justice Department's continued scrutiny of its activities.

Industry watchers know full well that a year earlier, Microsoft may have been able to successfully strong-arm Intel out of making an investment in Red Hat. In addition to bringing it a presence in a promising new market, Intel's investment in Red Hat also gives it enormous new leverage over Microsoft.

This fact does not seem to be lost on Microsoft, which continued its attempts to dampen the attention on Linux. Prior to Intel's worldwide launch of its Pentium III processor, Red Hat and Intel had worked for months to present an impressive demo for the occasion that would be featured in major cities around the world. The two were working to demonstrate a Pentium III machine running Red Hat Linux and a Ben & Jerry's e-commerce application running on software from Oracle.

Shortly before the event, Microsoft made sure to "kill" the demo and pressured Intel into replacing it with Windows NT running the same application. Intel executives regrettably informed Red Hat of this shortly before the launch date.

What's more, during the DOJ's trial, while Microsoft was disparaging Linux in the marketplace, it was ironically using it to defend its position to the feds that it did not control a monopoly.

Microsoft, during the trial, presented an internal Microsoft memo noting with apparent alarm that a rival operating system, Linux, is outselling Microsoft's Windows in some retail channels. Microsoft's lawyer cited the memo to show Windows faces growing competition.

"Recently in CompUSA, Microcenter, and Fry's, Linux is outselling Windows 98," and retailers are reaping bigger profit margins on the products, the May 25 email between Microsoft executives said.

"I object!" shouted an irate David Boies, the government's lead attorney, who complained the document was not appropriate evidence because it was developed during the course of the trial by Microsoft employees.

Judge Thomas Penfield Jackson allowed the Linux memo into evidence, but called it "self serving," seeing that it was created as the trial was going on, another seemingly disingenuous ploy by the software giant, who suddenly found it of benefit for its legal position to extol the success of Linux.

But the government's witness, Massachusetts Institute of Technology economist Franklin Fisher, pointed out that most users get Windows preinstalled on PCs, while most people get Linux at retail.

When given the chance to re-examine his witness, Boies returned to Linux, reading several public statements from Microsoft executives, with some as recent as March 1999. They describe Linux as no threat to Windows, and in one from June 1998, Gates notes that the Linux following should remain small.

Microsoft's concern with Linux was again clearly illustrated when two company memos were leaked to Eric Raymond back in November 1998, who posted them on the Internet. They became known as the Halloween documents. In them, Microsoft engineer Vinod Valloppilil wrote, "OSS [open source software] poses a direct, short-term revenue and platform threat to Microsoft. The ability of the OSS process to collect and harness the collective IQ of thousands of individuals across the Internet is simply amazing."

He went on, noting that software of "commercial quality can be achieved/exceeded by OSS projects."

Valloppillil and Josh Cohen, another Microsoft developer, then compared the performance of Microsoft's Windows NT and Internet Explorer with Linux and Netscape Navigator, two open source products, on the same computer. They concluded, "The combination of Linux/ Navigator ran at least 30 percent to 40 percent faster when rendering simple HTML [the text and commands on Web pages] plus graphics."

The second memo stated, "Linux's hacker orientation will never provide the ease-of-use requirements of the average desktop user." But that was the precise goal of the Gnome project, and of companies like Red Hat, SuSE, and others.

***

While Linux use was growing in the U.S., it was catching on like wild-fire in Asia. Linux users, including Japanese Broadcasting Corp, HSBC Securities Japan Ltd., an office supplies firm Otsuka Shokai group. Linux is also used in large-scale research projects, notably at Tokyo's Rockefeller University.

In the spring of 1999, a string of announcements from Japanese companies threw more weight behind Linux. In March, Fujitsu Ltd. said it will begin selling servers based on Linux; and both IBM Japan and NEC Corp. announced plans to begin offering Linux support services.

Software companies Trend Micro and JustSystem said they would also enter the Linux market. JustSystem said it would support Linux with a release of its ATOK12 software, which supports Japanese text entry, and the popular Ichitaro word processor for the Linux platform. For its part, Trend Micro, the Tokyo-based anti-virus company, said it would launch a version of its InterScan Virus Wall software for Linux.

Fujitsu, linking up with affiliate PFU Ltd., will offer a Linux sup-port service focusing on the company's Granpower 5000 server. The company said it would provide Linux installation and other services, and would support both Red Hat and TurboLinux versions of the op-erating system.

NEC, Japan's biggest personal computer maker, announced its first tentative steps into the Linux market with plans to begin offering in-formation on the Web on the compatibility of its systems with Linux.

IBM Japan said it would begin supporting RedHat and Turbo Linux distributions following the lead of its U.S. parent. In addition to working on running Linux on its Netfinity PC servers, IntelliStation workstation, and Thinkpad notebook PC, the company is also working on a release of its DB2 Universal Database for Linux.

Linux was only beginning to appear on the radar in that market niche. And it too was growing like wildfire.

Bake Off

"What a ride. And the remarkable part is that it's just beginning."

—Bob Young, CEO of Red Hat, Inc.

THE FIRST TIME THE IDEA OF GOING PUBLIC came up was in the middle of our January 1999 board meeting. A drama had unfolded. At our Triangle Park offices in North Carolina, I sat with Marc Ewing, Frank Batten Jr., Benchmark's Kevin Harvey, Bill Kaiser of Greylock, and our new president Matthew Szulik.

As we discussed our next investment round, slated for March, that would result in funding from IBM, Compaq, Novell, Dell, SAP, and Oracle, Bill Kaiser interrupted with a startling idea.

"Why don't we just scrap that investment round, and go straight to a public offering?" Kaiser suggested. "Why raise several million dollars from these companies, when we can make a leap and raise a much larger number of dollars in the public markets?"

I was a skeptic at first about the idea of an IPO at all. As an occasional reader of *The Economist* magazine and a self-proclaimed entrepreneur, I had been regularly annoyed that the magazine assumed that for any new technology to succeed in the marketplace, the suppliers of that technology had to eventually gain access to the resources available from the capital markets.

What about all those Horatio Alger stories of people who started in their garages and built great companies without outside financial support? What about SAS Institute, a brilliantly successful billion-dollar corporate software developer built over the past 25 years by Jim Goodnight, just down the road from us in Cary, North Carolina? It didn't have any outside investment support.

My idealism about doing everything on our own slowly shifted during a series of meetings that began with the gathering of our board. The demand for support and services by major industry players from IBM to Compaq to Dell dwarfed our ability to supply those services.

The board members were silent for a moment mulling Kaiser's startling pronouncement. Kevin Harvey agreed with Kaiser that, even back in January, a Red Hat offering would have been well-received.

Forty-one-year-old Matthew Szulik, who at that time had been president and COO of Red Hat for only 60 days, then brought everyone back on track. "Even if the market is ready for us, we're not ready for the market," he protested.

Szulik had been involved with several technology companies, including MapInfo, that had gone public and had seen the difference in their success once they were prepared to face the shareholders demands for consistent financial results in the years after their public offerings.

He was also aware of an idiosyncrasy of the IPO process: The investment banks who were courting us would be enthusiastic and supportive until they had sold all the shares in our IPO. The day after the IPO, their allegiance would switch to their other clients, the pension funds and other investors who bought the shares.

If the company did not achieve everything that it claimed it would during the selling of the IPO, the investment analysts would be the first to point this out to the market and the value of the company's shares would plunge. Customers and suppliers might then be reluctant to purchase products and services from the company out of concern it might not be around to support the products in the future.

Companies without a strong and experienced management team prepared for these pressures frequently suffer dramatically at the hands of a skeptical investing public. Successful companies are ones that are well prepared and use their public offering as a springboard to greater success.

In January 1999, Szulik felt Red Hat was not ready on all these counts. We resolved to go ahead with the investment round. In order to have a credible story for the public markets we had to have more support from the industry. We could not go public until we had a much more tangible set of commitments from a set of partners and until we had built an even stronger management team. (For readers baffled by the IPO process, see Appendix A for a brief primer.)

We had to get endorsements not only for what we were doing but for the whole open source model as well, if we were going to have any shot at convincing the capital markets that Red Hat wasn't just a hackers commune, which many journalists had depicted.

The board decided to proceed with the March investment round and to use the resources from that round to build up our management team and our management information systems, as well as to fine-tune our business model so that we would be in a position to consider a late-summer IPO.

A word of warning for anyone considering an IPO. Don't.

It reminds me of nothing so much as one of those multilevel video games with hidden dangers and Byzantine rules. It is also very hard work. It is fraught with pitfalls at every turn. Fortunately, we had very talented help throughout the process, from our bankers, lawyers, and accountants, particular the team at our lead underwriter, Goldman Sachs.

The best example of these challenges is our experience trying to get some of the shares we were selling in the IPO to the programming community who had helped build many of the tools we were using in Red Hat Linux.

First, Donnie Barnes spent three weeks scouring the Internet, digging up all the contributors lists to all the open source projects he could find. He came up with a list of almost 5,000 people—the first time anyone had ever attempted to compile a comprehensive list of open source contributors.

Of course, his list was in no way comprehensive, as the vast majority of open source software contributors did so only casually, when they had a need or the available time to contribute. As a result, such contributors did not get their names registered in the key contributors lists that Donnie was researching. But it was still a much more comprehensive list than anything previously compiled.

Then we had to craft a letter to this list of developers. The Securities and Exchange Commission (SEC) has a complex set of rules of what companies can and cannot say when they offer shares to the public. If you don't stay well within the rules, the SEC can (and regularly does) simply withhold permission to proceed with your IPO. I'm sure they have very important and well researched reasons for implementing each and every one of these rules. But to the companies who have to negotiate these rules on their way to a public offering, the rules appear designed solely for the purpose of ensuring the mental collapse of anyone who attempts to navigate through them.

For example, we were in the SEC-imposed quiet period. This is one of the more bizarre notions to a salesman like me. How can you sell shares in your company if you are not allowed to promote your company for three months before your IPO or for another month after your IPO? In the letter addressed to the developers, we could describe the offer, but not mention any reason why anyone should want to accept the offer. That would be promoting the shares in the quiet period—a big no-no, according to the rules.

So we ended up with a letter which, while legally acceptable, was sufficiently badly worded to end up alienating a significant percentage of the developers we mailed it to.

And the SEC has a set of rules to govern who is eligible to purchase shares in an IPO. First you must be a U.S.-based taxpayer to buy IPO shares that are listed on an American exchange. So this eliminates the eligibility of half of developers we had wanted to send the offer to.

The SEC also has a set of rules designed to protect the public from scam artists who use public stock offers to con inexperienced investors out of their money. In effect, the SEC deems IPO offers to be extremely high-risk investments and therefore buyers of shares in IPOs must prove that they are experienced investors who can afford to lose the money they are being asked to invest.

Unfortunately a not insignificant percentage (about 15 percent, as it turns out) of the developers we were offering shares to were either still students, or otherwise inexperienced investors by the SECs definition.

And, of course, since the offer was not actually made by the SEC but made through Red Hat and E*Trade, when members of the development community (to whom we had originally extended the offer) found themselves declared ineligible, they naturally blamed us and E*Trade.

Fortunately for both Red Hat and E*Trade, the members of the open source development community are a bright and well-informed group. Within days, if not hours, the real story of the problems and challenges imposed by the SEC rules and regulations surrounding public offers were quickly disseminated throughout the developer community. The general commentary was grateful to Red Hat and E*Trade for at least attempting to get IPO priced shares into the hands of the development community.

The final result was that well over a thousand open source developers where interested, eligible, and able to participate in our IPO.

———————

As it turned out, our business model benefited the most from the March investment round, and got us in good shape for an IPO at a later date. We worked closely with Intel, Compaq, Dell, IBM, Novell, Oracle, and SAP to determine exactly what it was that they, and their customers, were looking for.

Between January and April, momentum continued to build. After all, it takes time for corporations to decide to deploy a new operating system. People who adopt operating systems recognize they're making a long-term commitment. The catch was that we, as a small company, had focused in the first few years on the "early adopting" technical user. We knew the enterprise user wasn't going to come anywhere near an operating system whose biggest single supplier comprised a small team of engineers down in the tobacco fields of North Carolina.

For that reason, with the backing of the likes of IBM, Compaq, and Dell during our C series of funding, we gained a lot of credibility. The Intel/Netcape deal had also served to create the understanding that industry leaders had given our product their seal of approval.

The endorsements from Dell, Compaq, and IBM cemented the perception that Red Hat Linux was a technology on which reliable, multibillion-dollar companies were going to build products.

What we learned from partnering with these giants was that although we were giving away a complete state-of-the-art operating system without license restrictions of any sort, the best business model turned out to be exactly the same as the one for companies who sell software with license restrictions. That is, most computer users do not want to take full and ongoing responsibility for the technology they are using. They want to buy solutions to their business problems from companies who have the resources to help determine what those solutions are, and who can deliver and support those solutions. In effect, most customers don't want to buy technology at all. If they could get away with it, they'd still be using quill and ink.

Technology, however does make radically better business solutions possible. Red Hat had to have the resources available, through financing, and the staff and skills to deliver great products to the customers of Compaq, Dell, and IBM that would enable them to build more robust information systems. We had to provide complete support so that they would be worry-free about the operating system that made their solutions possible.

Red Hat's Linux product development team, and testing, quality-control and documentation teams, were enabling us to supply better technology, but we needed to build the customer support and services teams. Our goal was to turn technology into better solutions for the scores of customers our new partners were introducing to us.

As an example of the management team we are building, we brought in Charles Coleman to head up the acquisition and implementation of a set of enterprise systems for the company. He helped us select Oracle's enterprise-level tools for that job. We had been using the very capable Appgen accounting database tools, but had simply outgrown their ability to support the large and rapidly growing company we were becoming. Oracle assured us that it would take only six months to get Red Hat switched over to the Oracle business solution. But, as we told them, we did not have the luxury of six months.

We pushed the notion of "Red Hat time" to Oracle. The Internet was allowing companies to operate much faster than was previously possible in "normal time." At Red Hat, we had always recognized that to take on companies as large and successful as Microsoft, we were going to have to move faster than they did. We could not operate on normal time, nor even in Internet time, but at a pace we called "Red Hat time."

Red Hat time required that Oracle install its software so that Red Hat would be able to run its business within 30 days. At first, Oracle executives laughed at the idea. But to their credit, and our ongoing gratitude, we were able to meet that goal in only 37 days—the fastest implementation Oracle had ever accomplished.

This new system enables us, among other things, to track all of our customers as individuals so that we can offer advanced subscription services to customers of our Red Hat Linux products. That is, if a customer buys a version of our product, we'll give them access to premium services.

This may sound easy, but in our case we have several million users of Red Hat Linux and have to track each one. Because of the high cost of talking to each one individually, we have to automate our interactions with customers and put this information on the Internet. This way, customers can log in and get access to the special services that they need from among the wide range of services offered.

This is the kind of thing that Amazon.com does every day. However, it had a four-year head start on that level of sophistication, which in large part was made possible through funding from capital markets. Amazon.com has been able to take what it does and translate that on a very large scale. That's the kind of scale we have to operate at if we're going to service the needs of major accounts.

There are no guidelines for weighing the right time for a public offering. Gauging this is more a combination of what a company needs to do to get to the next level, what resources are needed for greater success in the marketplace, and whether the application of those resources benefits the company in the short run. Equally important is to determine the most effective way of raising the capital needed. When a company needs to raise money, it can issue notes or bonds—known as debt securities—or stock, known as equity securities.

In our case, we're a quasi-Internet stock. Clearly, the capital markets were receptive to funding a new business model of the sort that Red Hat's open source strategy represented. This was also attractive to us because the cost of raising capital through the public markets is lower than the cost of raising capital if we had gone to the bank, for example.

The situation is different for each company and each industry. For example, in the 1980s, I was in the computer leasing business in Canada, with a company named Vernon Rentals. At the time, the vast majority of companies in that business were bigger than we were in terms of revenue. Vernon Rentals going public made no sense at all because the banks were willing to finance the inventory we needed and the capital markets weren't particularly interested in us. In short, computer rentals is not a glamorous industry and is not perceived as a very high-growth industry.

In the case of Red Hat, the industry we're serving is growing as fast as any industry on the planet. It's the kind of industry in which the capital markets are very effective as a source of funding—they're visionary in terms of funding the potential of new companies and new industries.

As Warren Buffet has pointed out, he makes all of his money by buying stocks and putting them under his mattress for five years. By definition he's buying stocks in companies he believes have great long-term prospects. The capital markets, for all the reputation of day trading and the fickle swing of the Dow, are actually a very effective mechanism for funding new businesses and industries.

A bank, on the other hand, has a set of conditions you must conform to and can call its loan and put you in bankruptcy if you don't meet each profitability target. By selling stock in the capital market, your investors are directly or indirectly making a much longer-term bet on the outcome of your company and your industry. We are a relatively small company but we are clearly in an industry that has a huge amount of upside potential.

A Red Hat IPO would represent the first opportunity for the capital market to weigh in on whether this open source software movement is for real. If the capital markets decide Red Hat is for real, and they're willing to fund us, it would have a self-fulfilling impact. The capital raised would help ensure Red Hat was a success, fulfilling the market's prediction.

Going public would enable our company to raise more money and at a lower cost than it can through debt offerings. This is true for most companies. Of course, you can use junk bonds or quasi-junk bonds that can represent a fair amount of capital, especially these days with interest rates being so low. However, as a general rule, it's easier and costs less to raise money as equity, and it's a longer-term play. That is, management can focus on longer term planning because having already raised equity, the available corporate funds are not going anywhere.

With our C round of financing complete and lots of new business in the works, Red Hat was going like gangbusters. By April we concluded that Red Hat was ready to consider an Initial Public Offering.

We were ready for a "bake-off"—in the lingo of Wall Street, the ritual of selecting an underwriting team from the various investment-bank suitors. With all the publicity that Linux, Red Hat, and the open source movement had received, major investment banks had been lobbying us aggressively for our business. They had assumed that we would eventually be filing an IPO and wanted to make sure they had the inside track on our business. I was so besieged by all the top investment banks, in fact, that I used to discourage them.

So when the board discussed which investment bankers we should consider inviting, and which might be interested in taking us public, it was a simple and short discussion.

The DoubleTree Inn in Raleigh, North Carolina, just down the road from Red Hat's offices was beginning to fill up with a gaggle of suits, the top investment bankers in the world.

It was May 1999, and only a week had passed since Red Hat had placed a call to Goldman Sachs and Morgan Stanley Dean Witter & Co. Both had eagerly agreed to compete for Red Hat's business as the lead underwriter for the company's IPO. Selecting the two leading investment banks was consistent with our goal of partnering with the best suppliers available.

The Goldman Sachs and Morgan Stanley teams each flew in on separate corporate jets, and the executives stepping off those planes that day represented a veritable Who's Who on Wall Street.

From Goldman Sachs & Co., which had some 50 professionals assigned to its Internet banking group, the cream of the crop came. There were Lawton Fitt, a managing director; Lawrence Calcano; Rick Sherlund, ironically the analyst who had followed Microsoft since the day Goldman had taken the company public; and Michael Parekh.

Goldman Sachs was a most hallowed name. It had handled Yahoo's stunning IPO. When Goldman Sachs took Yahoo public in 1996, it was almost an object of ridicule. At the time of the IPO, Yahoo's market cap was about $300 million. Today, it's about $30 billion.

In 1996, members of Goldman Sachs' technology banking group held an electronic tour of the Web and then had a debate about e-commerce and the market for Internet initial public offerings.

That early brainstorming paid off well. Goldman Sachs emerged as the dominant player in the stock market's hottest sector. It has underwritten eleven Internet IPOs worth $986 million since January 1996, according to Securities Data Co.—more than double that raised by Hambrecht & Quist Group Inc., the San Francisco company that is Goldman Sachs' closest competitor.

Goldman Sachs is also the leader in Web mergers and acquisitions, having been brought in on fourteen deals worth some $14.4 billion. Since 1996, it has enjoyed about $108 million in fees from these deals.

Morgan Stanley's team was equally strong. Even though it ranks fifth in IPO volume since 1996, it has underwritten several of the Internet market's largest secondary offerings, including those of Netscape and America Online. With such deals and other merger and acquisition work, Morgan Stanley's Internet group has attracted $63 million in investment banking fees—more than any firm other than Goldman Sachs, according to Securities Data.

Morgan Stanley was also attractive because it had Mary Meeker, considered Wall Street's top Internet analyst. Internet-related stocks are difficult to evaluate because the companies usually have little revenue and no earnings. Picking winners can be a perilous endeavor. Investors often rely on analysts, which in turn prompts companies looking for an IPO to hire investment banks with the best analysts. Morgan Stanley was the underwriter for Netscape's IPO in August 1995.

Red Hat held a board meeting shortly after the Goldman Sachs and Morgan Stanley presentations.

At the meeting the choice was clear. We chose Goldman Sachs to lead the Red Hat IPO, which both Goldman Sachs and Morgan Stanley assured us would be one of the more exciting IPOs of the year.

In the ensuing weeks, Goldman Sachs' Fitt and others worked on setting the offering price with us. Setting this price is a balancing act as well as an art. If the price is set too low, the stock could go through the roof in the public market once shares start changing hands. In such a case, privileged investors who got in at the offering price make out like bandits. However, the company that's going public receives only a small fraction of the proceeds it might have had. If the price is set too high, the company takes home a lot of money, but its stock could quickly plummet below the offering price as trading continues, resulting in negative publicity and unhappy investors.

For years, underwriters have used a general rule of thumb: Value the deal so that the stock will jump about 15 percent on the first day of trading. However, in recent years with the hot IPO markets, underwriters have been known to set prices low and let stocks leap 50 percent and sometimes even double.

Currently, in the summer of 1999, we are a $10.7 million company looking to raise about $100 million. Retail sales accounted for 70 percent of our business the previous year, in addition to software sold via our Web site and by a small direct-sales team.

Last year we lost roughly $130,000 on about $11 million in revenue, a tiny loss compared with those suffered by most Internet start-ups. We're planning to ramp up our service offerings. Last year, software sales were 93 percent of our business, and services accounted for the rest.

Red Hat Linux accounted for 55 percent of all Linux-based operating systems sales in 1998, according to International Data Corp. Training, education, customer support, consulting services, and e-commerce will provide the bulk of our future profits.

Early on, we recognized that our competition has never been with other open source operating system suppliers, but rather with Microsoft and to a lesser extent with IBM, SCO Unix, and Sun's Solaris.

In order to deliver to our customers the services they're going to need in order to use these technologies properly, and to deliver to the industry and all the independent software vendors such as Oracle and SAP the services they need to build sophisticated applications for Red Hat Linux, we have to have quick access to capital that we're unlikely to generate off our own operating revenue in the short term.

In our eventual S1 meeting, we would seek to raise about $96.8 million in the IPO. By comparison, in our private rounds of funding, we raised an initial $2 million from our angel investor Frank Batten Jr., followed by the $8 million we raised in September 1998 with the investments from Greylock, Benchmark, Intel, and Netscape. Series C raised another $7 million in March of 1999 from Compaq, IBM, Dell, Novell, and Oracle.

With our IPO we would actually be selling roughly 10 percent of the business to the new investors who would buy the IPO shares. In May of 1999, our valuation estimated by Goldman Sachs was between $800 million and $1.2 billion dollars. The market capitalization would be based on the IPO price.

We had pondered the risks involved in doing the deal, and decided they were few. It wasn't likely that the capital markets would cool in general toward technology stocks. We didn't foresee much bad news in Internet stocks between June and the end of July. If the market did cool, our valuation might be reduced slightly, but it would not eliminate the offering.

We did consider what Microsoft could do to us, as an exercise. For example, a week before our IPO was to register, what if Microsoft were to fund a whole bunch of little developers to sue us claiming ownership of some piece of the code we were shipping. That could scare some investors who might believe such suits had some merit. Of course, it would be an unbelievably bad PR move for Microsoft, unless it conducted such activity via one of its stealth campaigns. Fortunately, with the Internet, Microsoft's stealth campaigns are getting more exposure than they would have otherwise.

But we weren't particularly concerned about Microsoft in the next quarter or two. Ironically, as long as the Justice Department has Microsoft in the spotlight, it needs a competitor. They need to be able to go to Judge Jackson and say this has no merit because we're not a monopolist. If Red Hat went public at a billion-dollar market capitalization it implies that there is some competition occurring in the marketplace for server operating systems.

Of course, even going public at a billion dollars means Red Hat has a tiny fraction of Microsoft's market capitalization. That's not very formidable competition. We would be one-quarter of one percent of Microsoft's size in terms of market value.

We recognized, however, that if the Justice Department backs off the case or settles, there's no question Microsoft could do some very evil things to us. But, again, the reason we have longer term confidence is because we're delivering unique benefits to the marketplace that Microsoft simply can't afford to offer. They could certainly hurt some of our short-term prospects, but it can't hurt our long-term opportunities.

———

Working through the logistics of our IPO, which was filed on June 4, 1999, we benefitted from expert advice by Kevin Harvey, Bill Kaiser, and others at Benchmark and Greylock. Their experience suddenly made us an old hand at performing such a complicated deal. We were no longer a little upstart company in North Carolina. We were being shepherded by industry superstars.

The experience of Eric Hahn was also a boon. Hahn had joined our board in the spring of 1999, and he had a lot of insight into the IPO journey from his past experience with other companies, including Netscape.

By the summer of 1999, Red Hat was ready for its road show. Everything appeared to be going smoothly with the SEC, and Goldman Sachs was ready to make its pitch to the public.

During Red Hat's road show, we would again outline our vision for the future. Open source does three things for us. Our strategy is like a three-legged stool. First, it enables us to build better technology and do it at a significantly lower cost than the proprietary software vendors. The economies of scale normally work in favor of the biggest suppliers, and as you get bigger, the cost per unit of shipping your product keeps going down.

The increasing dominance of Microsoft makes the barriers to entering the market increasingly greater for small innovators. But what this open source cooperative development model has allowed us to do is to turn on their head the economies of scale for building operating systems. Suddenly it was possible to build better operating systems than even the biggest technology companies at a fraction of the cost.

Second, open source allows us to deliver unique benefits to our customers: For the first time the customer has control of the operating system. Customers can look under the hood, and are no longer beholden to their supplier for getting new features, patches, or bug fixes. Customers can rely on one supplier, hundreds of suppliers, or they can fine-tune the operating system themselves.

Third, the business opportunity with open source is huge, it delivered benefits to everyone in the industry from IBM to Intel, from major corporations to individuals working in their basements. From the beginnings of Red Hat, the question was always: How big is the opportunity, how will we know when we are successful?

Finally, in the case of Red Hat, we're in the operating system business and every computer on the planet needs an operating system— every application requires one.

In the past there were many "anyone but Microsoft" efforts: OS/2, Taligent, and so on, but most of them never got off the ground. What always struck me was, for the first time, open source software represented an operating system that would not pose a competitive threat to hardware or software companies in the industry because Red Hat will not control their destinies quite the way a vendor of a proprietary operating system supplier can.

You can think of an operating system as being the infrastructure of the computer industry in the same way that the highway system is the infrastructure of the trucking industry. The problem with Microsoft is it owns that highway and can charge whatever toll it wants. Worse than that, it can change the direction of the operating system highway to suit its applications, putting its competitors and customers at a disadvantage by changing APIs and file formats.

With Red Hat Linux, we're the maintenance company. We're the guys who change the light bulbs, repave the highway, plow the snow, but we can't actually do anything to the highway without the full support of the software development community that we work with in order to build that highway.

In the early days, I thought: If everyone really hates Microsoft, we've got the perfect solution. And yet back in the time between 1993 and early 1995, attempting to convince companies such as IBM that this was going to be a solution to their operating system needs would get us laughed out of the room. We recognized the fact that we had to prove the concept in the market place.

When you add these three aspects together you realize this is a massive opportunity.

People will insist that going public will put new pressures on Red Hat and change the culture at the company. But business, whether public or private, involves challenges. You see a lot of public companies complaining about the pressures of the public markets forcing them to do the wrong thing. In the late 1970s and early 1980s, that was a theme in American business. The myth was the Japanese were running circles around us because the Japanese investors had a long-term view of life and American investors had a very short-term view of life.

For their book *In Search of Excellence*, Tom Peters and Robert Waterman studied a dozen highly successful American companies, only to find there was basically no truth to the accusation. In fact, the truth was that Japanese companies were simply better managed at that time. The successful American companies were running circles around their Japanese competitors. And they didn't have to complain about the short-term focus of capital markets or the fact their workers didn't have a work ethic or didn't do calisthenics in the morning. They just figured out how to do what they needed to do to be successful in the marketplace. Then they just went out and did it.

These companies were very disciplined about how they went about their businesses. And that's very much Red Hat's philosophy and the reason for our success to date. We do what our customers need us to do and with a long-term focus.

Relative to other companies in its category, Yahoo has been able to maintain an incredibly high valuation because each and every quarter it delivers on the analysts' forecasts. In other words, Yahoo forecasts carefully and provides real value to its customers and shareholders. And it delivers more than predicted. That's a sign of a well-disciplined, carefully run company.

Are there traps and pitfalls associated with being a public company? Yes, but they're well known and understood. The trick to staying away from these pitfalls is to plan with detail and execute carefully.

Some wonder whether going public will influence our commitment to the open source model. Keep in mind that it's our customers who influence us the most. That's where our commitment to open source comes from. At the same time, I won't predict the future. We want to serve our customers, not our own personal ideologies.

———

Most of the general business principles important in my journey with Red Hat—management do's and don'ts, trusting your co-workers, being honest and forthright, and so on—I had previously learned in the tough computer rental and leasing business earlier in my career.

The unique factor in the Red Hat adventure is the opportunity to change the industry.

I've always been fascinated by business and free markets. Although business executives have a reputation for being conservative, the fact is that most of the major social trends of the last millennium have been either initiated or enabled by business men and women. It was business people who financed the deployment of all the great inventions that have reduced hunger, improved medicine, and raised incomes worldwide.

Red Hat's opportunity is to fundamentally improve the way software is developed. Although the programming community understands that sharing source code is a better way to develop software, it was business considerations that prompted IBM and other companies, beginning in the early sixties, to withhold source code from the users of their products.

According to my theory, the people who are going to solve this "problem" on behalf of the programming community are going to be other business people. They will invent business models that will enable them to succeed because they deliver unique benefits to their customers as a result of including source code with their products.

It is frequently those companies that deliver the biggest benefit to society that also become extremely successful as a result. WalMart delivered high-quality goods at an extremely low cost and both its customers and its shareholders benefit from this. Bell Telephone (AT&T) improved the efficiency of business everywhere by deploying a telephone network, and both the users of the phones and the shareholders of Bell Telephone benefited as a result.

If Red Hat can have a fraction of the positive impact those companies have had on our society, our customers and our shareholders should be pleased with the result. This opportunity is the reason I often find myself commenting, "Having this much fun at work, and getting paid for it, should be illegal."

―――――

As we discussed, our shareholders to date have all invested in Red Hat because they believed in what we were doing with open source, not despite it. Their investments are enabling us to do more of the same.

Our public offering will be for only a small percentage of the company, so I expect control of the company will remain the same. At the same time, we expect that most of our new shareholders will be equally supportive of our business model, provided we are able to make the sort of return on investment that we are projecting.

I expect we will be encouraged to improve our business model, or the board will find a management team that is able to do that. In any case, everyone recognizes that we are not going to able to compete with Microsoft under the industry's current proprietary, binary-only model. This is why Red Hat's loyalty to the open-source software model is assured regardless of who is calling the shots at Red Hat at any point in time.

―――――

Marc Ewing and I can only shake our heads. In little more than four years, we've gone from selling Linux out of our homes (to avoid getting real jobs) with few ambitions for great financial success, to being fought over by the world's two largest investment banks during our IPO.

On August 11 we found ourselves on the trading floor of Goldman Sachs watching Red Hat stock begin trading. The success of our IPO even surprised the veteran executives at Goldman. We expected to see some interest in RHAT, our trading symbol on the NASDAQ exchange, but we were thrilled by the avalanche of orders. The price of the stock soared from $14 to $52 on its first day.

Regardless of the short term swings in our stock prices, clearly, the Linux and open-source arenas are in their infancy. All we see is growth. Selling free software has gone from an activity that labeled us as unrealistic dreamers to being referred to as industry visionaries.

What a ride. And the remarkable part is that it's just beginning.

Appendix A:
Understanding The
IPO Process

W HEN A COMPANY NEEDS TO RAISE MONEY, it can issue notes
or bonds—known as debt securities—or stock, known as equity
securities. Anytime new stock is issued, it comes from "Authorized But
Not Yet Issued Stock." This is called a Primary Offering, if the company
has sold stock before. A company can have many Primary Offerings. If
the company has never sold stock before it is known as an "Initial Public Offering."

The first step for the company is to hire an investment bank, which
will be known as the underwriter. Underwriting is the actual process of
raising capital through debt or equity. The investment bank will act as
the advisor and the distributor, although it does not necessarily need
to be used to raise capital. If they so choose, companies can go door to
door selling their bonds or stock on their own. But investment banks
are almost always used.

The chosen investment bank and the company need to discuss and
negotiate a variety of things, including the amount of capital needed
by the corporation, the type of security to be issued, the price of the

security, any special features of the security, and the cost to the firm to issue the securities. Once agreement is reached, the investment bank acts as the middleman between the corporation and the general public.

Two different types of agreements exist between the investment bank and the company. With a firm commitment agreement, the investment bank agrees to purchase the entire issue from the corporation and then offer it to the general public. With this type of an agreement, the investment bank has guaranteed to provide a certain amount of money to the corporation. The risk of the issue falls entirely on the investment bank. If it fails to resell the amounts of securities it purchased, the investment bank still has to pay the agreed upon sum of money to the corporation.

A best efforts agreement, on the other hand, means that the investment bank agrees to sell the securities for the corporation but does not guarantee the amount of capital raised by the issue.

When a company makes a public offering it must comply with the Act of Full Disclosure, which is part of the Securities Act of 1933. Red Hat had to file a Registration Statement, which is filed by the investment bank with the SEC. The day the investment bank turns in the registration statement with the SEC is known as the filing date.

This registration statement includes a description of the business raising the money, biographical material on the officers and directors of the company, the amount of shares owned by each insider—which includes officers, directors, and shareholders owning more than 10 percent of the securities; complete financial statements including existing debt and equity securities and how they are capitalized; how the funds will be used; and any legal proceedings involving the company (for example, strikes, lawsuits, antitrust actions, copyright/patent infringement suits). The firm must also disclose whether it is aware of impending or future actions.

After the registration statement is filed by the investment bank on behalf of the issuing corporation, the SEC requires a "Cooling Off

Period," sometimes called the quiet period. During this time, the issue is considered as "In Registration," and the SEC investigates and ensures that the company has fully disclosed all pertinent information. The quiet period was at one time 20 days, but currently takes much longer. Once approved by the SEC, the stock will be offered to the general public. The day that this happens is known as the "Effective Date." If the SEC does not approve the issue, a "Letter of Deficiency" is issued, which informs the company what was wrong. If such a letter is issued, effective date will be postponed.

During the quiet period, the investment bank will also try to drum up interest in the issue by distributing a "preliminary prospectus," which is also known as a "red herring." This is because it has red printing across the top and in the margins. The investment bank pays for the printing of the red herring, which introduces the general public to the corporation. The red herring contains much of the information from the registration statement including a description of the company, a description of the securities to be issued, the company's financial statements, the company's current activities, the regulatory bodies overseeing the company (if any), the nature of the company's competition, who the company's managers are, and how the funds from the issue will be used.

The public offering price and the effective date are not contained in the red herring and are not known throughout the quiet period. On the effective date, the offering price is officially established, set in keeping with current market conditions.

During the quiet period, the investment bank may not provide any other information to its clients other than what is contained in the red herring. For example, it can't provide research reports, recommendations, sales literature, or anything from any other firm about the company.

During the quiet period, if the investment bank's clients are interested in the issue, the clients will give their stockbrokers, who work for the investment bank, an "Indication of Interest." The stockbroker does not take an order for the issue from the client, who can only indicate interest. The higher the indication of interest is from clients, the better for the offering. In fact, it will usually help the investment bank in making pricing decisions.

Just before the effective date, the investment bank will have a due diligence meeting with the company going public to resolve any last minute concerns and make sure no material changes have taken place between the registration date and the effective date.

Once the effective date arrives, the security can be sold and money collected. In addition, the final prospectus is issued, which is very similar to the red herring but includes the missing numbers for the public offering price and the effective date.

If an investment bank doesn't want to take on all the risk of an IPO by itself—which happens often—it can form a "syndicate," a group of investment bank underwriters who will participate in selling the issue. Usually, the Syndicate Manager or Underwriting Manager is the head of the syndicate. The underwriting manager will then sign a letter of intent with the issuing corporation to formalize the relationship. This is a non-binding arrangement. Once the SEC has approved the issue, all parties to the agreement sign a contract that binds them to the letter of intent.

The three primary underwriting contracts include the agreement among underwriters (AAU), the "underwriting agreement" (UA), and the "Dealer Agreement." The AAU is an agreement that establishes the relationship between the underwriters. It designates the syndicate manager to act on their behalf. The syndicate manager is the one who determines the public offering price, enters into the underwriting agreement, modifies the offering price (if necessary), determines when to make the offering, responds to deficiency letters by the SEC, modifies the selling commission, and controls all advertising. The Underwriters Allotment is the amount of the security each underwriter agrees to purchase.

The UA is a contract that establishes the relationship between the corporate issuer of the securities and the underwriters comprising the syndicate (or just one underwriter if there is no syndicate). The UA is executed by the managing underwriter based on the authority it has been given by the AAU.

The Dealer Agreement (or selling agreement) is a contract that allows securities dealers who are not part of the syndicate to purchase some of the securities from the issue. The underwriters may not be able to locate enough purchasers for the issues, so they can approach other securities dealers to invite them to participate. These other securities dealers may have even been offered a chance to participate as an underwriter but chose not to. These additional securities dealers help move the stock to the general public. Basically, they are another distribution channel. However, these securities dealers are free from risk. The Dealer Agreement allows them to purchase the securities at a discount from the offering price in order to fill client orders they may have received after the effective date.

All of this is the case if a firm commitment is involved. However, with a best-efforts underwriting, there is no syndicate. The underwriters don't make a commitment to purchase the securities: instead, they merely agree to do the best they can in selling the issue. In this case, the underwriters form a selling group. Each participant in the underwriting does his best to sell his allotted share of the issue.

One other form of underwriting agreement exists: it's known as All Or None. In this case, the underwriter agrees to do his best to sell the entire issue by a certain date. All of the proceeds go into an escrow account. If the securities are not all sold by the certain date, the money is returned to the purchasers and the issue is canceled.

Appendix B:
The Lazy Programmer
Theorem

THE QUESTION:
Why has the Linux OS grown more unified and consistently stronger over the course of its seven year history, while other high profile cooperative software projects (BSDs, Unixes, JAVA) have been subject to unproductive splitting of the cooperative development teams?

The Hypothesis:
A truly freely re-distributable license is more important to the cohesiveness of the Linux OS than any other factor including: the remarkable leadership shown by key players in the Linux space, lessons developers have learned over time, necessity, or any other single factor.

The Data:
Specifically there is the mystery as to why the Linux kernel and most of its core surrounding components have not balkanized into dozens of separate implementations all promoted by competing developers.

Linux development projects, and other GPL'd code, have a very unified development history. There are no sustained forked projects of any GPL'd code, despite changes in leadership, heated debates, and frequent discussions of this possibility. The only significant fork we can find is the old (1997) fork of the glibc libraries into the glibc and the libc versions. But as a classic exception that proves the rule, the merge of these projects back together again leaves us without a lasting example.

The UNIXes, Java, and the BSD's, have a history of forking, and of ongoing development of the various increasingly divergent forked projects. UNIX is copyrighted under the old AT&T license, and has resulted in [many versions]. Various pieces of UNIX licensed under more liberal terms have shown much more cohesion including the X Window System, Sendmail, and many others.

JAVA from SUN Microsystems is a brilliant example of code that is forking despite the massive costs of maintaining separate versions of the language for reasons that are all due to the desire for competitive advantage—and—the fear of the other companies contributing to the promotion of JAVA of losing control of the platform to a single contributor to the project. (i.e., SUN itself)

The Theory:
Maintaining software code is more expensive than writing it, which is the reason that software projects do not normally fork.

In order for software projects to fork there must be two conditions:

One—the copyright under which the code is licensed must both allow and enable other programmers to fork the code.

Two—the copyright under which the code is licensed must provide an incentive for programmers to wish to undertake the effort to fork the code and assume the ongoing expense of maintaining the code.

The cost to maintain a program is greater than the cost to write it, and a code base will only fork if and when someone determines that the benefit of the fork outweighs the cost of maintaining the fork. Which, of course, is not terribly original. All sorts of studies show, usually in real dollar terms (but the point is the same), that the cost to purchase software and hardware (develop it), is a tiny fraction of the cost to use it (maintain it). The balance is so far off, in fact, that in most cases it is much less effort to work with someone who is already committed to maintaining the program to get your changes made.

Our Theory Restated:

Programmers are lazy, therefore forks are rare. The Incentives to fork software projects come in a variety of forms:

I. Competitive concerns—that one member of the project will benefit more from the work of the group than the other members. e.g.: JAVA, where SUN's control of the project encourages other system vendors to fork the project.

II. License Restriction Concerns—that a contributor to the project would like to use the code for purposes not specifically allowed for under the existing license terms.

III. Timing Concerns—Simple personal rivalries between competing development teams (BSD) create suspicions that improvements by one team will not be make available to the others at all, or even on a timely basis (which in the fast moving world of technology is the same thing).

None of these incentives work in the case of truly freely re-distributable software, where any improvements by any group will be available to any other group on a consistent and timely basis. While alternative projects have grown up and competed the better technology quickly wins greater acceptance.

This outcome fits our observations as well as our expectations, but more on both of those below.

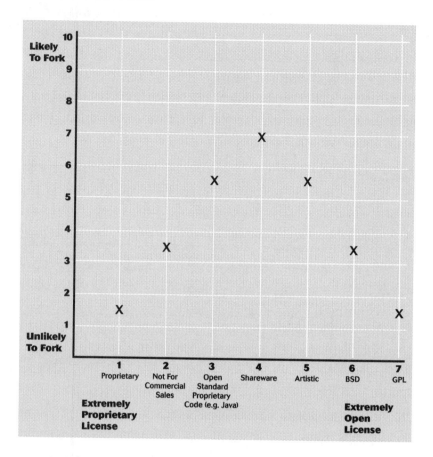

The Conclusion:

Software projects will not fork in situations where they cannot fork, and software projects will not fork in situations where there is no benefit to any group in assuming the cost of maintaining the forked code.

About The Authors

Robert Young

In just four years, Bob Young has taken Red Hat, Inc. from a fledgling start-up company to the leading global supplier of the Linux operating system. With 20 years of computer industry finance and marketing experience, Robert saw an opportunity with a phenomenon called Linux in 1993. He subsequently founded a Linux distribution and catalog business that later merged with Marc Ewing's organization to form Red Hat, Inc.

Wendy Goldman Rohm

Wendy is an award-winning investigative journalist and author of the best-selling book, *The Microsoft File: The Secret Case Against Bill Gates*, which recently won a "Best Nonfiction Book of 1998" award in the United States and has been published around the world in nine different languages. For more than a decade, Wendy has been a writer for numerous magazines and newspapers, including *Wired, Upside, Red Herring, Interactive Week, The Chicago Tribune, Boston Globe, Los Angeles Times*, and others.

Index

Other CORIOLISOPEN™ PRESS Titles

Linux Install and Configuration Little Black Book

ISBN: 1-57610-489-3
$24.99 U.S. • $36.99 Canada

Provides detailed solutions to installing and configuring the latest Red Hat and Caldera versions of Linux. Details the how-tos of partitioning hard drives, creating user accounts, working with file systems, networking, ISP connectivity, Xwindows, and more. Also covers hot new technologies like Gnome and Samba and how they relate to configuring Linux.

Linux System Administration White Papers

ISBN: 1-57610-474-5
$29.99 U.S. • $43.99 Canada

This collection of works by leaders in the Linux community presents the theoretical concepts, as well as the architecture, behind the Linux kernel. Topics covered include file systems, directories, boots and shutdowns, printing, TCP/IP networking, network management and configuration, security, electronic mail, and much more. A Foreword by Eric Raymond is included.

Linux IP Stacks Commentary

ISBN: 1-57610-470-2
$39.99 U.S.
$58.99 Canada

Contains over 500,000 lines of code with accompanying explanations. Covers Linux network stack and code, including the General Network Layer, the Core Services Layer, the Network Protocols Layer, and the Device Drivers Layer. Includes extensive cross-referencing and architectural flow charts.

Linux Core Kernel Commentary

ISBN: 1-57610-469-9
$39.99 U.S.
$58.99 Canada

Line-by-line, the Linux core code is examined and explained. The five main subsystems of the Linux kernel—Memory Manager, Virtual File System, Process Scheduler, Network Interface, and Interprocess Communication—are covered. Extensive cross-referencing enhances understanding of the structure of the code.

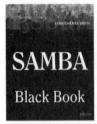

Samba Black Book

ISBN: 1-57610-455-9
$49.99 U.S. • $73.99 Canada

Details the smooth operation of a heterogeneous network, involving Linux and Windows. Covers the latest available version of Samba (Version 2) and includes information on installation, network management, file sharing, firewall and network security, network Internet connectivity, ftp servers, and network file and print servers. Troubleshooting tips are also provided.

Open Source Development with CVS

ISBN: 1-57610-490-7
$24.99 U.S. • $36.99 Canada

Learn the best practices of open source software development with CVS—a tool that allows several individuals to work simultaneously on the same document. CVS is covered in detail, as is the GNU license, software design and development, coding styles, documentation procedures, testing, release of software, and troubleshooting.

The Coriolis Group, LLC   Telephone: 800.410.0192 • www.coriolis.com
Coriolis books are available at bookstores and computer stores nationwide.